Isla

A C

DATE DUE

OCT 3 0 2000		
OCT 1 0 REC'D		
FEB 1 8 2002		
MAY 1 0 2003		
NOV 1 2 2008		

Demco, Inc. 38-293

Islam

A Concise Introduction

Neal Robinson

GEORGETOWN UNIVERSITY PRESS
Washington, D.C.

Georgetown University Press, Washington, D.C. 20007

First published in 1999
by Curzon Press
15 The Quadrant, Richmond
Surrey, TW9 1BP

Printed in Great Britain

Library of Congress Cataloging in Publication Data

Robinson, Neal, 1948–
    Islam, a concise introduction / Neal Robinson.
      p.   cm.
    Includes bibliographical references (p.   ) and index.
    ISBN 0–87840–224–1 (pbk.)
    1. Islam. 2. Islam–Doctrines. 3. Islam–Essence, genius,
nature. I. Title.
BP161.2.R59   1999   98-54856
297–dc21   CIP

In memory of my grandparents
George and Nellie Pettit

Contents

Preface

On numerous occasions, people in various walks of life have asked me to write a simple book about Islam. This work should appeal to them and other general readers. Nevertheless, it is aimed more specifically at would-be students. In many colleges and universities, course tutors are required to recommend preparatory reading to be undertaken during the vacation. Despite the ever-increasing number of introductory texts on Islam, there is none which really meets their needs. They know from experience that if they prescribe a book which is too long or too technical, the majority of their prospective students will not read it. On the other hand, they are understandably reluctant to recommend briefer works written by popularizers or apologists. I have tried, therefore, to produce something which is concise and relatively simple but not simplistic. Those with no previous knowledge of Islam will, I hope, find that it provides them with a panoramic view of the subject and whets their appetite for study.

Introductory courses on Islam often focus primarily on the classical period and deal in turn with the life of Muhammad, the Quran, the Hadith, Islamic law, theology, Shiism and Sufism. I have therefore discussed these important subjects relatively briefly, giving just enough information for the lecturer to build on. On the other hand, I have devoted much more space to subjects which feature only marginally in many lecture courses. For instance, there are two historical chapters ('Islam in History' and 'Islam in the Modern World') which should help students see the development of Islam in perspective, and four chapters on worship ('Ritual Prayer', 'Zakat', 'Ramadan', and 'The Pilgrimage') which should help them appreciate it as a living faith.

It is not possible to study Islam in any depth without encountering Arabic proper names and technical terms. In order to make these appear less forbidding to the novice, I have used a simplified system of transliteration. For example, I transliterate the name of the Prophet's cousin and son-in-law as Ali, rather than ʿAlī, and the term for 'religious scholars' as *ulama* rather than ʿ*ulamā*'. The more accurate system, together with several others which are in circulation, is explained in Appendix I, where the reader will also find some useful hints about the structure of Muslim names. Moreover, accurate transliterations of the more important names and terms are furnished in the indices. Another bugbear for the beginner is the profusion of unfamiliar dates. I have tried to lighten the burden by using bold type to distinguish key dates, which the reader should attempt to memorise, from others which are included for future reference. Events are dated in accordance with the common era in order to facilitate correlation with European and American history. Nevertheless, the Islamic calendar is explained in detail in Appendix 2.

The Quran comprises 114 suras each of which is subdivided into ayas. In order to save space, I have frequently referred to quranic passages rather than quoted them in full. For example, 42.3 indicates the third aya of the forty-second sura. The numbering system is that of the standard Egyptian edition, which is employed in most modern translations (but see pp 71–2). Apart from quranic references, which are usually given in brackets, I have deliberately eschewed notes except to indicate the sources of quotations. Moreover, in the bibliography I have included only a brief selection of books and articles which are relatively accessible. Needless to say, however, I have learned a great deal from other scholars who are not mentioned by name, including many whose works are more technical or are not available in English. I am also grateful to my students, especially those who ask awkward questions and offer constructive criticism of my courses. Alan Thacker read a first draft of the opening chapter and made some helpful suggestions. Finally, this book could not have been written without the constant support and encouragement of my wife Danielle.

Neal Robinson
The University of Leeds

List of Maps and Diagrams

What do you Know about Islam?

News Coverage of Islam

This book is intended for beginners. Nevertheless, it would be naive of me to assume that you had no previous knowledge of the subject. How could that be when the media bombard you daily with information about the Muslim world? With this thought in my mind, I decided to spend half an hour with a newspaper before settling down to write this opening chapter. It is Monday May 26 1997. The international news, on page 12 of today's *Guardian*, begins with a map of the Sudan and a large photograph of soldiers loading their automatic rifles on strips of cloth aligned like prayer mats in the desert. The caption reads, 'The Islamic state-in-the-making promises martyrs divine marriage with houris in paradise if they fight in the south', and the accompanying article about the Sudanese civil war is headed, 'Dark times loom for visionary Sudan'. At the foot of the page, there is a briefer article covering the election results in Iran. It mentions the struggle of the police to maintain dress and behaviour codes; during the post-election celebrations a woman was stopped in her car and arrested for wearing make-up, and schoolgirls (whom the Iranian authorities require to wear Islamic cover from the age of nine) discussed ripping off their head scarves. On the facing page the heading is, 'Taliban put neighbours on alert'. Beneath it there is another large photograph, this time of turbaned warriors aboard a battered truck in front of a domed mosque. The Taliban have now gained almost complete control of Afghanistan, and an earlier article in the same issue described how yesterday in Mazar-i-Sharif men doffed turbans and long shirts, while the few women who dared to venture outside their homes wore the one-piece head-to-toe *burqa*. The writer concluded, 'It is as if the country is being plunged back in time for the sake of peace'. Now, in this article, the focus is on the likely impact of the Taliban victory on the neighbouring central Asian states, which were until recently part of the Soviet Union. The words of a United Nations official are printed in bold type in a central panel, 'The fear is that you have five new states in search of an identity. Amid all their problems, one rallying identity is Islam'. The only other articles featuring Islam mention matters of more immediate concern to British citizens: two British nurses condemned to be beheaded under Islamic law in Saudi Arabia continue to plead their innocence, alleging that they confessed to murder under duress after being sexually abused by the police; and Mohammed Sarwar, the first Muslim Member of Parliament, is still resisting calls for his resignation in the wake of accusations of bribery.

As far as I am aware, none of the above information is untrue. Nevertheless, the cumulative effect of these newspaper reports is to project a distorted image of Islam as a backward and barbaric religion which is inimical to the values of western civilisation and which poses a threat to British citizens at home and abroad. There are three reasons why the image is distorted. First, all the articles which feature Muslims involve violence, repression, sexual immorality or corruption, and the two photographs combine martial and religious motifs. Nothing is said about situations in which Muslims live in peace, or about Islam's emphasis on charity and personal integrity. Presumably, such things are not considered newsworthy.

Second, the incidents which are mentioned are reported in a highly selective way. It is not made clear that there are many Muslims in the Sudan who do not support the National Islamic Front; that many of the young people in Iran who long for a less repressive regime nonetheless have no desire to reject Islam; and that in Afghanistan the majority of those who fought against the Taliban were themselves Muslims. Nor is sufficient emphasis given to the fact that Islam encourages the next of kin of murder victims to accept compensation rather than press for the death-penalty, and that if the two British nurses in Saudi Arabia are beheaded it will be because of the hardness of heart of their alleged victim's non-Muslim brother in Australia. As for the scandal surrounding the newly-elected MP for Govan in Glasgow, there is no mention of the reactions of Britain's Muslims, many of whom feel that he has disgraced not just himself but them and the whole of their community.

Third, the articles do not furnish the readers with the historical background which they would need in order to see these current affairs in perspective. The roots of the Sudanese civil war reach back to the colonial period, when the British exacerbated ethnic and religious divisions by closing the south of the country to the Arabic-speaking Muslims from the north and giving grants to Christian mission schools where pupils were taught in English. The present regime in Iran dates from the Islamic revolution which put an end to the tyrannical rule of the Shah in 1979. Because the Shah was pro-western and enjoyed the full support of the USA, the Islamic government has been staunchly opposed to western influences of any sort, not least the relaxation of conventions governing female modesty. The endemic instability in Afghanistan was made worse by the clash of western and Soviet interests during the Cold War. The USSR invaded the country in 1979 to prop up the communist government. The USA and Britain reacted by aiding the Mujahidin, who were a loose alliance of Muslim groups united in their opposition to communism. When Soviet troops finally withdrew in 1989, however, external support for the Mujahidin dried up and their former foreign backers encouraged factional fighting to undermine their attempt to establish an Islamic state. Nevertheless, in the face of near total anarchy they decided eventually to back the Taliban as the faction most likely to restore order. As regards Saudi Arabia, it is important to remember that the British and American economies are heavily dependent on the purchase of petroleum and the sale of armaments. Over the years, the Saudis have proved reliable suppliers of the former and avid customers of the latter. It has therefore been in Britain's and the USA's economic interest to turn a blind eye to the deficiencies of Saudi Arabia's judicial system, especially as the majority of its victims have been Saudi dissidents or migrant workers from the Third World. Finally, in the UK, Muslims have been present in large numbers since the nineteen-fifties and now comprise a significant minority, but the lack of proportional representation militates against Muslim candidates being elected to Parliament. There is much more to the background to each of these four situations, but I hope that I have said enough to make you realise that Britain and the USA are not simply innocent spectators of events in the Muslim world.

A History of Misrepresentation

It is worth pausing to ask why it is that the media image of Islam and Muslims is predominantly negative. A simple answer might be that western society requires external enemies and internal scapegoats in order to preserve its own cohesion and that, now that the Cold War is over, the Muslim world has inherited the traditional role of the Soviet Block, while Muslim immigrants bear the stigma formerly reserved for 'reds under the beds'. Although there is an element of truth in this, the reality is more complex. Over the past few decades, a number of militant Islamic movements have come into existence. The reason for their emergence will be explored in the course of Chapter 4. The fear and suspicion which they arouse is to some extent justified but the assumption that they have the support of all Muslims, and that they represent authentic Islam, is not. Moreover, negative views of Islam were prevalent in Europe before these movements saw the light of day. The origin and development of distorted perceptions of Islam form a long and fascinating story. Here I have space to evoke only a few of the more important episodes.

The roots of European hostility to Islam reach back to the seventh and eighth centuries, when Muslims conquered large parts of the Byzantine Empire including Syria, Palestine, Egypt and North Africa. The state religion of the Byzantine Empire was Orthodox Christianity, and Christian theologians like John of Damascus (d. before 753) responded to the loss of those territories, and the conversion of Christians to Islam, by developing a polemical approach to the new religion. They argued that Islam was the most recent and most pernicious of the many heresies which had beset the Church, and they portrayed Muhammad (may the peace and blessings of God be upon him) as a false prophet, the forerunner of the antichrist, who had acquired a garbled knowledge of Christianity through contact with an Arian monk. Despite gross distortions, the writings of the Byzantine theologians did contain some accurate information about Islam. It was known, for example, that in pre-Islamic times the Arabs had been pagans, and that Muhammad had taught them that there was only one God, although the polemicists gave him little credit for this because of his denial of the Trinity.

The situation in mediaeval western Europe was somewhat different. Apart from Spain, very little territory was lost to the Muslims. In fact, by weakening the Byzantine Empire, Islam strengthened western Christendom, for it gave the Frankish kingdom the opportunity to form a new Christian empire and it made it possible for the papacy to advance its claim to universal authority over the Church. In their isolation, western Europeans long remained almost entirely ignorant of Islam and assumed that the Muslims, or Saracens as they called them, were idolaters like the Slavs and other barbarians who lived beyond their borders. In 1095, when Pope Urban II summoned the European knights to launch the First Crusade, it is unlikely that any of those who responded knew or cared about the beliefs and practices of the people they vowed to fight. They simply assumed on the basis of the Bible that the Saracens were the descendants of Abraham's illegitimate son Ishmael and that Christians, as Abraham's true heirs, had a right to the Promised Land. During the period of the Crusades, more accurate information about Islam became available. A decisive step was made by Peter the Venerable, the Abbot of Cluny (d. 1156), who commissioned Latin translations of the Quran and other Arabic texts in a bid to defend the Church against Islam. The so-called Cluniac Corpus, which was produced in Spain, included an anti-Muslim tract called the *Apology of al-Kindi*. This had a section on the life of Muhammad, which contained details drawn from Islamic sources but selected for their polemical utility and presented in a hostile manner. Subsequent Mediaeval biographies of Muhammad, penned during the period of the Crusades and drawing on information derived ultimately from Byzantine sources, were written in a similar vein. They generally depicted him as an opportunist, an imposter, a lecher and a warmonger.

5

Despite widespread appreciation of Arab philosophy, medicine and science, the largely negative attitude to Islam as a religion persisted well beyond the end of the Middle Ages. The main reason for this was that Islam was the religion of the Ottoman Turks, and the expanding Ottoman Empire posed a serious threat to Europe and hence to Christendom. During the second half of the fourteenth century, the Ottomans overran a large part of the Balkans. In 1453, they captured Constantinople, the capital of the Byzantine Empire, and converted the cathedral church of Haghia Sophia into a mosque; in the sixteenth century they conquered Hungary, besieged Vienna, and made two abortive attempts at taking Malta; and as recently as 1683, they were again at the gates of Vienna.

Towards the end of the seventeenth century, when Ottoman power was visibly waning, Europeans began to visit Muslim countries in increasing numbers as diplomats, merchants and travellers. At the same time, more scholars began to treat the Muslim world as a serious field of study. A Frenchman, D'Herbelot, compiled what amounted to the first encyclopedia of Islam, the *Bibliothèque Orientale,* which was published posthumously in 1697. Despite D'Herbelot's admiration for Islamic civilisation, however, he did not question the received wisdom that Muhammad was an impious impostor who founded a false religion. Nevertheless, as the European Enlightenment progressed, attitudes began to change, especially amongst those who were less enamoured of Christianity than D'Herbelot had been. Islam was sometimes haled as a rational religion akin to the Deism of the Enlightenment philosophers. Many educated people admired the fact that Muslims were egalitarian; that Islam preached a comparatively healthy attitude to sexuality; and that the Ottomans had proved extraordinarily tolerant towards religious minorities such as Jews and Protestants. These educated people included the historian Henri de Boulainviliers (d. 1722), who wrote a full-scale biography of Muhammad, describing him as a great statesman and a profound political thinker and lawgiver, who founded a religion which fostered reason, justice and tolerance.

European admiration for Islam, which was widespread during the Enlightenment, was shared by Napoleon Bonaparte. Unfortunately for Muslims, however, his short-lived occupation of

Egypt, which lasted from 1798 to 1801, heralded the advent of the colonial period and the eventual incorporation of most of the Muslim world in the French, British and Dutch Empires. The effect of this on European perceptions of Islam were both positive and negative. On the positive side, great advances were made in the study of Arabic, and key Islamic texts were edited and translated; there were pioneering ethnographic studies like Edward Lane's *The Manners and Customs of the Modern Egyptians* (1842); and the drawings in David Roberts' *Egypt and Nubia* (1846–9) led to an appreciation of Islamic architecture. On the negative side, however, even the best European scholars in this period tended to exude an almost effortless superiority. Islam was, after all, the religion of subject peoples. Subject peoples are, it was supposed, inferior. Hence, the argument went, Islam is an inferior religion. Worse still, in the eyes of many European scholar administrators, Islam was actually the root cause of Muslim inferiority – an archaic system of beliefs and practices which stood in the way of progress and modernity. Although some held this opinion sincerely, others were not above employing double standards. For instance, Lord Cromer, the British consul general in Egypt, attacked Islam for its degrading treatment of women, while back at home he was a founding member and sometime president of the Men's League for Opposing Women's Suffrage.

The seclusion and veiling of women in Muslim societies had long been a subject of fascination for Europeans. From the end of the sixteenth century onwards, travellers had returned from Istanbul with anecdotes about the Sutlan's seraglio; and at the beginning of the eighteenth century, Galland had produced a bowdlerised French translation of the tales of *The Thousand and One Nights*. In the nineteenth century, however, the 'Orient' increasingly fuelled male erotic fantasies. Voyeuristic paintings of Muslim women in harems, slave markets and Turkish baths, became fashionable; Sir Richard Burton translated *The Thousand and One Nights* in full, adding detailed notes about the sexual mores of the Arabs; and writers like Flaubert escaped the ennuis and restraint of European society to look for inspiration in Egyptian brothels.

In addition to scholars, administrators, artists and writers, Christian missionaries played an important part in fashioning

7

the European vision of Islam during the colonial period. Many of them held views which were scarcely more enlightened than those of the medieval polemicists. Monseigneur (later Cardinal) Lavigerie, who became Archbishop of Algiers in 1867, argued that the French government should support the Church's attempt to convert Muslims to Christianity because this was the only way that such barbarians could be civilised, and in 1882 Muir translated the *Apology of al-Kindi* into English for the benefit of Protestant missionaries working in India.

Although, as we have seen, European perceptions of Islam during the colonial period were somewhat mixed, two events above all others reinforced the popular image of Islam as the enemy of civilisation. The first was the Greek War of Independence, which lasted from 1821 to 1829. For western Europeans, Greece was a symbol of both Christianity and classical culture. Hence European sympathies were with the Greeks as they fought against their Ottoman overlords, and essayists and poets alike picked up their pens to portray the latter in the blackest possible terms. The second was the First World War. At the outbreak of war in 1914, the Ottomans had little choice but to side with Germany. The Sultan called on Muslims to join him in *jihad* (holy war) against Britain, France and Russia. In the course of the war, Britain and her allies disseminated propaganda which vilified the Ottomans along with the Germans. Impartial historians have long recognised that the Germans were by no means as culpable as was alleged, but few have seen the need to put the record straight regarding the Ottomans.

Continuing Obstacles to Understanding

Since the end of the First World War, a number of distinguished Christian scholars have forged lasting friendships with Muslims and have worked throughout their lives to undo the harm caused by centuries of anti-Muslim polemic. The conciliatory statements issued by the Second Vatican Council in the mid nineteen-sixties are a measure of these scholars' success at the official level. The statement contained in the 'Declaration on the relationship of the Church to non-Christian religions' is particularly significant. It reads as follows

Upon the Muslims too, the Church looks with esteem. They adore one God, living and enduring, merciful and all-powerful, Maker of heaven and earth and Speaker to men. They strive to submit wholeheartedly even to His inscrutable decrees, just as did Abraham, with whom the Islamic faith is pleased to associate itself. Though they do not acknowledge Jesus as God, they revere him as a prophet. They also honour Mary, his virgin mother; at times they call on her, too, with devotion. In addition they await the day of judgement when God will give each man his due after raising him up. Consequently, they prize the moral life, and give worship to God especially through prayer, almsgiving, and fasting.

Although in the course of the centuries many quarrels and hostilities have arisen between Christians and Muslims, this most sacred synod urges all to forget the past and to strive sincerely for mutual understanding. On behalf of all mankind, let them make common cause of safeguarding and fostering social justice, moral values, peace and freedom.

(W. M. Abbot, *The Documents of Vatican II*,
London 1967, p. 663).

Nevertheless, this revolution in the Roman Catholic Church's official policy has been slow to influence the thinking of ordinary church-goers in Europe and America, many of whom still cling to the medieval notion of Islam as diabolic.

It is not only Christians who have difficulty in viewing Islam dispassionately. If anything, the problem is even more acute for western secularists. There are two closely related reasons for this. First, secularists feel uncomfortable with Islam because it challenges their assumption that religion is essentially a private affair which ought to have no place in the public domain. Second, they usually fail to appreciate why many Muslims have serious reservations about the desirability of an officially secular society. Looked at from the perspective of European history, and bearing in mind both the intermittent persecution of Jews in Western Europe and the wars of religion which were unleashed by the Protestant Reformation, it may seem obvious that separation of religion and state is the best way of guaranteeing religious freedom. To many Muslims, this is far from obvious, and here I must digress a moment and attempt to put their point of view. For over five-hundred years the Ottoman empire, which was a self-consciously Islamic empire, proved remarkably tolerant towards religious minorities. Although, under Islamic law, Jews and Christians were effectively second-class citizens, their lives and property were considered inviolable and they generally prospered. (The persecution of Armenian Christians in the nineteenth century and during the First World War, when the empire was disintegrating, was uncharacteristic). When, on the other hand, the European empire-builders annexed vast tracts of the Muslim world, their high-minded ideas about 'equality' and 'human rights' proved empty rhetoric. Likewise in the post-colonial period, Muslim countries such as Turkey, which opted for a European-style secular constitution, have often failed in practice to foster religious tolerance. Nor do Muslims living in France and Germany feel that they have genuine equality and security. This is hardly surprising when one reflects that they are frequently subject to racial discrimination but have virtually no voice in the democratic process, and that western governments recently did little to prevent the near annihilation in Bosnia of one of the oldest and most well-established Muslim communities in Europe.

Non-Muslim members of the public who are neither Christians nor convinced secularists also often have a negative attitude to Islam. This, one suspects, is mainly because of the way in which it is portrayed in the media – the subject with which this chapter began and to which we must now return. Today's *Guardian* was typical in largely neglecting the religious beliefs of Muslims and focusing on violent events in the Muslim world. It was, however, untypical in giving so much coverage to Sudan and Afghanistan. The media are normally more concerned with events which are likely to have an immediate effect on Europe or the United States. Because petroleum oil is vital to western economies, this means in practice that the oil-producing countries of the Middle East or their neighbours usually steal the limelight from the other less affluent Muslim states. Within living memory, the Middle East has been the theatre of a series of violent conflicts. It needs to be stressed that although these conflicts involved Muslims, they were not caused exclusively, or even primarily, by Islam; they were part of the legacy of European colonial intervention in the region. Let us look very briefly at the Arab-Israeli Wars and the Lebanese Civil War by way of example. It is impossible in a few sentences to do justice to the complex circumstances which gave rise to these events. Here, I wish simply to indicate certain indisputable facts about their historical origins.

From 638, when Jerusalem was captured by the Arabs, down to 1918 when the last Ottoman troops were driven out, the whole of Syro-Palestine was ruled almost continuously by Muslims. The only exception was a period of less than two hundred years, beginning in 1099 (with the conquest of Jerusalem from the Seljuks) and ending in 1291 (with the fall of Acre to the Mamluks) during which the Crusaders succeeded in gaining a number of tenuous footholds. Palestinians were therefore understandably hostile to rule by British Mandate and even more resentful when the modern state of Israel was established in 1947. Israeli expansionist policy has caused incalculable suffering to Palestinian Arabs and is a major factor in the continual tension which broke out into full-scale armed conflict in 1948, 1956, 1967, 1973, and 1982, and the *Intifada* (Arabic 'uprising') of Palestinians in Gaza and the West Bank in 1987.

After the First World War, when the League of Nations gave Britain control over Palestine it gave France control over Syria. During the nineteenth century, the Ottomans had created a separately-administered Christian area on Mount Lebanon and with this precedent the Arab Christians persuaded the French to divide the country into Syria and Lebanon. The division was opposed from the outset by Sunni Muslims in the area designated as Lebanon because they considered themselves to be Syrians. On the eve of Lebanese independance, which was achieved in 1944, the French mandatory authorities engineered a National Pact based on confessional proportionality. Parliamentary seats were divided between Christians, Sunnis, Shiites and Druze, with the Christians having a comfortable overall majority. Moreover, the pact stipulated that the President of the Republic was to be a Maronite Christian, although the less important posts of Prime Minister and Speaker of the House were allotted to Sunnis and Shiites respectively. This neat arrangement, which was intended to serve the interests of the economically-advantaged Christian sector of the population, worked well to begin with but was doomed to failure because it did not allow for demographic changes. Before long Muslims outnumbered Christians and were clamouring for a fresh census and a revision of the Pact. There was a brief uprising in 1958 when Lebanese Muslims with Arab Nationalist sympathies were outraged by President Shamoun's endorsement of the Eisenhower Doctrine on US intervention in the Middle East. The civil war which began in 1975 was much more serious and longlasting. It was ignited by a series of clashes between the (Christian) Phalangist militia and the Palestinian Liberation Organisation including the massacre of a bus-load of Palestinian refugees in a suburb of Beirut. It ended in 1989, when the National Pact was revised.

I have dwelt at length on the background to these recent episodes in the violent history of the Middle East in view of the role that they have played in perpetuating negative stereotypes of Muslims. Because the USA is geographically remote from the Muslim world and never colonised a major Muslim country, Americans are frequently more ignorant about Islam than their European counterparts. It is likely, therefore, that these events and others in the region have made an even greater impression on them than on Europeans. Nevertheless, it should by now be evident that although Muslims were involved in these events, the events themselves had little to do with their beliefs as Muslims. This inevitably raises the question, 'What is Islam?' – a question which I shall attempt to answer in the next chapter.

2 Defining Islam

Look at a map of the world and imagine yourself travelling eastwards from Morocco to Indonesia. The majority of the population in most of the countries which you pass through will be Muslims. This imaginary journey should make you aware that Islam is not simply the religion of the Arabs; in fact there are some 200 million Muslims in Indonesia alone, which is more than the total in all twenty-three Arab countries put together. It should also lead you to expect a good deal of variety in the beliefs and practices of Muslims. Were you to visit some of the countries too far north or south to be on your imaginary itinerary, you would encounter even more variety. Think for example of Turkey; or of Gambia, Guinea, Senegal and Mali in sub-Saharan Africa. Nor should the existence of all these Muslim countries blind you to the presence of substantial Muslim minorities elsewhere in the world. There are, for instance, over 100 million Muslims in India; at least 20 million in China; 6 million in the USA; 3 million in France; and 1 million in the UK.

I wish at this stage to introduce an important distinction between two adjectives which many authors use interchangeably: the adjectives Muslim and Islamic. When I speak of 'Muslim countries', I am using this expression as a convenient label for countries in which the majority of the population are for historical reasons nominally Muslims. There are, as we have seen, many such countries. As often as not, however, their regimes have little to do with Islam. Hence, it is misleading to refer to them as 'Islamic', thereby giving the impression that their constitutions have a thoroughly religious basis.

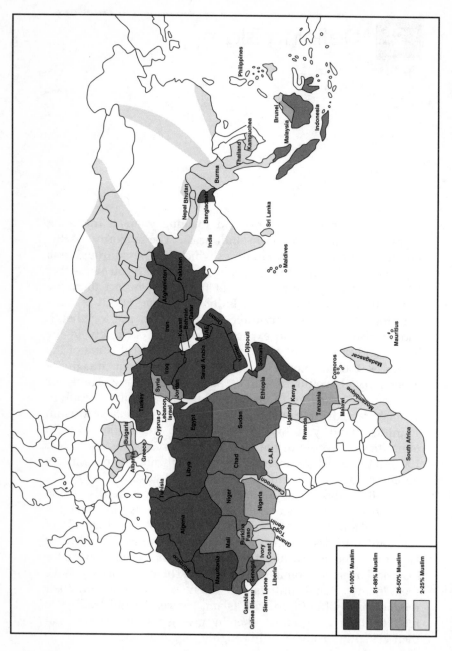

Figure 1 The Muslim World

Key:
- 89–100% Muslim
- 51–88% Muslim
- 26–50% Muslim
- 2–25% Muslim

So what is Islam? It is frequently said that it is the religion which originated with Muhammad, the seventh-century Arabian prophet. There are, however, several reasons why this definition needs to be qualified. In the first place, the root meaning of the Arabic word *islam* is submission or self-surrender, surrender being understood in the positive sense of recognising God's sovereignty and entering into his 'peace' (Arabic *salam*. For hints on the Arabic language see Appendix I). As such, **islam** seems originally to have denoted a personal act or attitude of mind rather than a religious system. Second, there is a *hadith* (saying of Muhammad) which implies that Islam is the natural religion of human beings

> Every new-born child is by nature a muslim. It is his parents who make a Jew, a Christian or a Zoroastrian of him. Likewise every animal is born whole. Have you ever seen one born with its ears clipped.
>
> (Robinson, *The Sayings of Muhammad* p. 13)

In Arabic there is no distinction between upper- and lower-case letters but the new-born child is clearly a 'muslim' with a small m, rather than a 'Muslim' in the sense of one who follows the detailed prescriptions of a specific religious system called Islam. Third, although the Quran implies that God perfected Islam as a religion during the lifetime of Muhammad (5.3), it also asserts that previous prophets including Abraham were muslims (2.128). Again, it seems appropriate to employ the lower-case m in this context, although we should note that the Quran elsewhere implies that the core beliefs and practices of all the prophets were identical with those of Muhammad. Fourth, within a century of Muhammad's death, Islam as a religious system had become the ideology of a vast empire which extended from Spain to India. In such circumstances, as is only to be expected, some relatively late ideas and practices were projected back and attributed to the Prophet and his Companions, although the extent to which this took place is of course hotly disputed. Finally, it is generally recognised that a number of developments took place in the course of the ninth, tenth and eleventh centuries, which gave Islam its classical form. These include the founding of the four Sunni law schools; the recognition of the Quran and the Hadith (prophetic traditions) as the primary sources of law; the emergence of Asharite theology; the hardening of the distinction between Sunnism and Shiism; and the establishment of *madrasas* (religious colleges) in which the curriculum was dominated by the study of Hadith and Islamic jurisprudence.

Muslims often speak of 'the House of Islam'. If it is legitimate to think of Islam as a building, then the Quran, the scripture revealed to Muhammad, is clearly its foundation. Extending the architectural metaphor, the Prophet said that Islam is built on five pillars, which he defined as: the *shahada*, or testimony that there is no god but God and that Muhammad is the Messenger of God; performance of the ritual prayer; compulsory almsgiving; the fast of Ramadan; and the pilgrimage to Mecca. These five pillars, raised on the Quranic foundations, support the whole fabric of the Sharia, the divine law. This architectural metaphor has the merits of highlighting the fact that Islam is a religion with a distinct and clearly-defined structure. It is, however, misleading insofar as it gives the impression that it is rigid and inflexible. To counter this and convey something of Islam's dynamism, I shall deal with 'Islam in History' and 'Islam in the Modern World' before looking in detail at the Quran, the five pillars and the Sharia. I shall also use the chapters on the two halves of the *shahada* to stress both the unity and the diversity within Islam. The difference between Sunnis and Shiites will be touched on in the chapter on 'Islam in History' but will be discussed at length in a final chapter on 'Denominations and Sects'.

3 Islam in History

Introduction

Most newcomers find the history of the Muslim world a daunting subject because of the seemingly endless list of unfamiliar names and dates. There is no way round this problem but I shall do my best to cut you a clear path through the jungle. Already, in the previous chapters, you will have encountered allusions to three famous Islamic dynasties: the Seljuks, the Mamluks and the Ottomans. In this chapter, I shall refer to many more (although the list will be far from complete!) situating them approximately in time and place. Before beginning, however, let me mention **SIX KEY DATES** to help orientate you. **In 622, Muhammad and his followers emigrated from Mecca to Medina**. This date marked a turning point in the fortune of the Muslims. It subsequently came to be regarded as the beginning of the Islamic era (see Appendix 2). **In 661, Muawiya, the first Umayyad Caliph, began to rule in Damascus**, thereby bringing to an end the twenty-nine year period of the four 'rightly-guided' Caliphs who succeeded the Prophet. Unlike the old capital, Medina, which was a desert oasis, Damascus had been part of the Byzantine empire and was an historic centre of Graeco-Roman civilisation. The Umayyads adopted many of its cultural and administrative traditions. **In 762, the Abbasids, who had overthrown the Umayyads thirteen years earlier, founded Baghdad as their new capital**. The move signified more than a change in dynasty. Baghdad was situated not far from the former capital of the Persian empire, and the consequent eastward shift in the centre of power led to the orientalization of the Muslim empire with the Caliphs ruling as eastern potentates. **In 1258, Baghdad was sacked by the Mongols.** Although the caliphal power had been severely restricted for a large part of the previous three centuries – first by the Persian Buyids and then by the Turkish Seljuks – the havoc caused by the Mongols was unprecedented. The destruction of Baghdad and the assassination of the Caliph came as a severe blow to Muslims everywhere and put an end to the classical period of Arab and Islamic civilisation. From this time onwards, the Muslim heartlands were dominated by members of various Mongol and Turkish dynasties. Of the latter, the last and most famous were the Ottomans. **In 1453, the Ottomans captured the Byzantine capital Constantinople**. This marked their coming of age as an imperial power and paved the way for their creation of a vast empire extending to the frontiers of Morocco and Persia, and spilling over into Europe as far as the gates of Vienna, which they twice besieged. **In 1571, the Ottoman fleet was defeated at Lepanto**, at the entrance to the Gulf of Corinth, by the combined forces of Venice, Spain and the Papacy. Although the empire survived into the twentieth century, this crushing defeat nevertheless ushered in its gradual decline.

In the rest of this chapter, I shall attempt to sketch the history of the Muslim world to the end of the seventeenth century. Although I shall devote most of the space to the rise and fall of dynasties, it is important to bear in mind that **Islam did not extend solely by military conquest**. It is undeniable that the rapid expansion of Islam, which took place within a century of the Prophet's death in 632, was facilitated by the military prowess of the Arab Muslims who stepped into the power vacuum left by the Byzantine and Persian Empires which were exhausted from fighting each another. Nevertheless, in some of the provinces of these empires, **Islam was welcomed because it held out the promise of a more egalitarian society and was more tolerant towards religious minorities**. In the subsequent expansion – especially in the Indian subcontinent, sub-Saharan Africa and south-east Asia, two other factors played an important part: **Islam was spread by Muslim traders and by Sufi *tariqas*** (mystical fraternities). Consider for instance the Indian subcontinent. Muslim troops entered the Indus valley and conquered Multan in 713; from the tenth century onwards, subsequent Muslim invaders succeeded in establishing various local dynasties; finally, in the sixteenth century, the Mughals united the whole of North India under Muslim rule. This, however, is only part of the story because Arab traders brought Islam to the west coast of India in the eighth century, and Sufi masters, such as Muin ad-Din Chishti (d. 1236) who settled in Ajmer, converted many poor Hindus by their simple lifestyle and emphasis on the love of God. Finally, it is a remarkable fact that **in some periods Islam was propagated by converts who belonged to previously non-Muslim dynasties**. For example, although the Mongols who sacked Baghdad were pagans, some of their Muslim descendants facilitated the spread of Islam in Russia and China.

The Mission of Muhammad (610–632)

Muhammad was born in **Mecca**, an important commercial and financial centre situated amidst the barren rocks of Arabia on the trade routes from Yemen to Syria and from Abyssinia to Iraq. Most of its inhabitants belonged to the Quraish tribe which was subdivided into a dozen autonomous clans. The city owed its prosperity to the possession of the well of Zamzam, and a sanctuary in which bloodshed was forbidden. In the heart of the sanctuary stood the Kaaba, an ancient cube-shaped building which Muslims believe was built by Abraham and his son Ishmael who dedicated it to the worship of God. By Muhammad's time, however, Ishmael's descendants, the Arabs, had lapsed into polytheism and the Kaaba was encircled with idols.

In 610, when Muhammad was about forty years of age, he began to receive revelations. He was commissioned to warn his people to abandon their idolatry and greed, and to urge them to worship God alone. In 622, because of increasing hostility to his preaching and threats to his life, he and his followers emigrated from Mecca to **Medina**, a fertile oasis 200 miles further north where he already had many supporters. Two thirds of the population of Medina were drawn from two Arab tribes, the Aws and Khazraj, who between them comprised eight clans. In addition there were three clans of Jews. Feuding was endemic and a few years earlier there had been a civil war in which Jewish loyalties had been torn between the two rival tribes.

Most sectors of the Arab population welcomed Muhammad's arrival in Medina, seeing in him a strong leader who could heal the divisions within their society. Although the Muslims who emigrated with him were drawn from several different clans, the Medinans looked on them as a single clan with him as their chief. His political status was therefore that of one clan chief among many. In addition, however, he was recognised as 'the Messenger of God', who received revelations applicable to them all, and before long the revelations began to refer to all the believers as constituting a distinct community. His position was further enhanced by his military role leading expeditions fighting 'in the way of God'. After a number of skirmishes with the Meccans – at Badr in 624; Uhud in 625; and Medina itself, which the Meccans and their allies besieged in 627 – he conquered Mecca in 630 and purged the Kaaba of idols. By this time, although in theory still chief of a 'clan', he was in effect the politico-religious leader of Medina. The Jewish clans had been driven out one by one, the last of them being liquidated in punishment for collusion with the Meccans during the siege of Medina. Moreover, Muhammad's reputation was such that whole tribes from elsewhere in the Arabian peninsula sent deputations seeking alliances with him. Later the same year, he led a massive expedition north to Tabuk near the Gulf of Aqaba. On the way, he guaranteed protection to Jewish and Christian communities in return for payment of a per capita tax known as the *jizya*. This policy, which was sanctioned by Quranic revelation, was the norm in Muslim societies up until the colonial period, and proved remarkably successful in promoting religious tolerance.

The First Four Caliphs (632–661)

When Muhammad died in 632, Islam had spread through much of the Arabian peninsula and the Muslims were poised to win more far-flung victories. His death without a male heir and without universal recognition of a designated successor, therefore precipitated a political crisis. There were four interest groups: the *Muhajirun* or Emigrants, who were the early Meccan converts, many of whom came from the Hashim clan to which Muhammad himself belonged; the *Ansar* or Helpers, who had rallied to Muhammad's cause in Medina; the late Meccan converts (the majority of whom belonged to the Umayya clan, Hashim's traditional rival) who had held out against Muhammad until the conquest of Mecca; and finally, those who believed that Muhammad had in fact designated his cousin and son-in-law Ali to succeed him. This last group were the forerunners of the Shia, literally 'the Party' – short for *Shiat Ali*, Ali's Party. After discussions **Abu Bakr** (632–4), an aged and revered Emigrant, who was the father of Muhammad's favourite wife Ayesha, was elected head of the Islamic community. Abu Bakr was styled Caliph (literally 'deputy' or 'successor') of the Messenger of God. He subdued the bedouin tribes who had renounced their allegiance to Muhammad after his death. He himself died in 634, but not before he had designated **Umar** (634–44), another Emigrant and long-standing friend of the Prophet, to succeed him. During Umar's reign the Muslims conquered large parts of the Byzantine Empire – including Syria, Palestine and Egypt – and overthrew the Persians. The two key battles were the defeat of the Byzantines at Yarmouk in 634 and the Persians at Qadisiya in 637. Umar's generals built garrison towns at Kufa and Basra, in Iraq, and Fustat (now part of Cairo) in Egypt, which functioned as bases for further military expeditions. When he was murdered in 644, the six men whom he had chosen to deal with the succession elected **Uthman** (644–56). Although Uthman was an Emigrant, he belonged not to the Hashim clan but to the Umayya. He proceeded to appoint members of his own clan as provincial governors and to bestow on them lands which had previously been the property of the state. This caused widespread dissatisfaction which led ultimately to his assassination in 656. **Ali** (656–61) was elected to succeed him but was unable to overcome the opposition of his rivals. In particular, Uthman's cousin Muawiya, the governor of Syria, blamed Ali for the assassination and refused to swear allegiance to him. Ali moved his capital from Medina to Kufa in Iraq and confronted Muawiya in battle at Siffin. The battle was indecisive and Ali decided to accept arbitration. This displeased the bedouin tribesmen who had fought at his side, and one of them subsequently assassinated him.

Sunni Muslims regard the period of the first four Caliphs as a golden age and refer to them as *rashidun* or 'rightly-guided' Caliphs. Shiites, on the other hand, consider Abu Bakr, Umar and Uthman to have been usurpers.

The Umayyads (661–750)

After Ali's assassination, his elder son Hasan tried to succeed him but Muawiya persuaded him to renounce his claim to the Caliphate. Muawiya, who had been the governor of Syria for twenty years, himself became Caliph almost without opposition, and transferred the capital to Damascus. Shortly before he died in 680, he nominated his son Yazid to succeed him, thereby founding a dynasty. By this time, Ali's elder son Hasan had died peacefully in Medina. Those who opposed Yazid's succession therefore rallied to the support of Hasan's brother, Hussein, the Prophet's only surviving grandson. He and seventy of his followers were slaughtered by Yazid's troops who engaged them in battle at Karbala. Yazid was succeeded by twelve further Umayyad Caliphs. The normal pattern was for the ruling Caliph to nominate his successor during his lifetime and to have him acclaimed by representatives of the main groups of Muslims, thereby preserving the fiction that he was chosen by consensus. Whereas the first four Caliphs had been 'Caliphs of the Messenger of God', the Umayyads styled themselves 'Caliphs of God' and understood this to mean that they were viceroys appointed by him. They adopted many of the administrative and courtly practices of the Byzantines, and under them the empire expanded westwards to incorporate North Africa and Spain, and eastwards as far as the Indus valley.

The Abbasids (750–1258)

A revolution which began in Khurasan, in eastern Persia, and was backed by disgruntled non-Arab peoples in the conquered territories, as well as by the supporters of Ali's descendants, led to the overthrow of the Umayyads. They were replaced by the Abbasids, a dynasty who belonged to the Hashim clan and claimed descent from Abbas, one of the Prophet's uncles. **In 762, al-Mansur, the second Abbasid Caliph, founded Baghdad as his new capital**. It was built on a circular plan probably as a symbolic representation of the world. The positioning of a mosque and palace in the centre indicated the Caliph's role as cosmocrator. For three hundred years the arts and sciences flourished under Abbasid patronage and there were important developments in theology and jurisprudence which gave Islam its classical form. Apart from the almost immediate loss of Spain, the borders of the empire at first remained virtually static, but from the middle of the ninth century onwards the empire began to disintegrate. Before long, the Caliph's effective political control extended barely beyond Iraq; the other territories were either lost to rival dynasties or were ruled by 'Sultans' (an Arabic word which simply means 'holders of power') who owed only nominal allegiance to Baghdad. From 945 until the twelfth century the Caliphs were little more than puppets in the hands first of the Buyids, who were Shiites, and then the Seljuks, who were staunch Sunnis. After a brief revival of Abbasid fortunes, **Baghdad was finally sacked by the Mongols in 1258**, and al-Mustasim, the last Caliph to rule in that city, was murdered. Although this event shook Muslims everywhere, it did not completely put an end to the Abbasids. Their fate will be mentioned later in connection with the Mamluks.

Islam in Spain (711–1492)

The history of Muslim Spain (*al-Andalus*) is closely linked with that of North Africa (*Ifriqiya*). The invasion of the North Africa began during the reign of Umar in 642, immediately after the conquest of Egypt. In 670, the Umayyads established a garrison town in Qairawan (now in Tunisia) which they used as a base from which they pressed further west. In 711, having completed the conquest of North Africa, they crossed over into Spain near Gibraltar (Arabic *Jabal Tariq*, 'Tariq's Mountain') which is named after Tariq b. Ziyad, the general who led the invasion. Apart from the north-west, **most of Spain was under Muslim control by 715**. From there, the Arab forces penetrated France but their progress was checked by Charles Martel who defeated them at

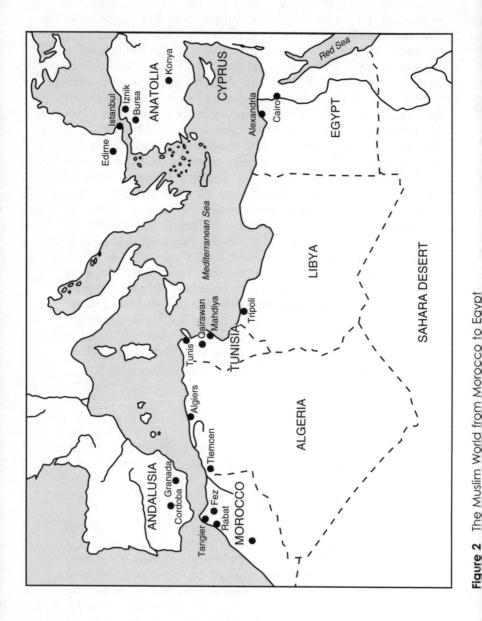

Figure 2 The Muslim World from Morocco to Egypt

Poitiers in 732. When the Umayyad dynasty fell to the Abbasids in 750, a solitary survivor of the massacre fled from Damascus to Spain where he established an independent dynasty. These **Spanish Umayyads (756–1031) ruled in Cordoba**, a city which soon became as prosperous and culturally advanced as Abbasid Baghdad. From 929 onwards, members of this dynasty styled themselves Caliphs, thereby indicating that like the Fatimids (see below) they saw themselves as rivals of the Abbasids.

During the decline of the Spanish Umayyads and after their final collapse, there was a period of political fragmentation which saw the emergence of no fewer than twenty-three local dynasties known as **'Party Kings'** (1009–1091). By this time, the Christian *reconquista*, which had begun in the second half of the eighth century, was making a headway. It was checked when the **Almoravids** (Spain 1090–1145; North-West Africa 1056–1147), a Berber dynasty who had ruled North-West Africa independently since 1056, crossed into Spain in 1086 and suppressed the Party Kings over the next few years. The Almoravids recognised the Abbasid Caliphs as the spiritual leaders of Islam. Their name is derived, via Spanish, from the Arabic *al-murabitun*, 'those who dwell in frontier monastery fortresses', a word which has also given us *marabout*, the French term for a Muslim holy man or hermit. The Almoravids ruled Spain from the Moroccan city of Marrakesh, which they had made their capital in 1062. However, their success against the Christian forces was short-lived. In 1118, they lost Saragossa and by 1145 they had withdrawn from Spain almost completely. While the Almoravids were losing control, some of the Party Kings re-emerged as independent rulers, but most acknowledged the suzerainty of the **Almohads** (Spain 1171–1212; North Africa 1130–1269) another North-African Berber dynasty. The Almohads (Arabic *al-muwahhidun*, 'those who affirm God's unity') were the followers of Ibn Tumart (d. 1130) a puritanical reformer and self-proclaimed Mahdi – a messianic figure expected to establish justice near the end of time. When he died, his lieutenant Abd al-Mumin declared himself Caliph and established the Almohad dynasty, conquering Morocco and making Marrakesh his own capital in 1147. Almohad troops invaded Spain in 1171 and captured Seville the following year. At the height of their power, the Almohads held sway over southern Spain and the whole of North Africa east of

Tripoli. In Spain, however, they could not hold out for long against the *reconquista*, and a decisive defeat in 1212 caused them to withdraw. Local Muslim rulers with Almohad sympathies retained limited control for a few more decades but Cordoba was lost in 1236, Seville in 1248, and most of their remaining territories over the next twenty years. The last Muslim foothold in Spain was the little kingdom ruled by the **Nasrids** (1231–1492). This was founded by a man of Arab descent who gained control of the area around Jaén in 1231, and seized Granada in 1235, making it his capital. There his descendants held sway for more than two and a half centuries until in 1492, the year in which 'Columbus sailed the ocean blue', they were forced to surrender to Ferdinand and Isabella of Castille.

The Fatimids (909–1171) and Buyids (932–1062)

At the end of the ninth century, when the whole of the Middle East was troubled by Shiite agitators, propagandists claimed that Ubaydallah, an alleged descendant of Ali and the Prophet's daughter Fatima, was the Mahdi. Ubaydallah came from Syria to North Africa which he rapidly brought under his control. In addition, his sympathisers occupied Sicily. He took the throne name al-Mahdi, and his capital (situated on what is now the Tunisian coast) was appropriately called Mahdiya. The third Caliph, al-Mansur, had his own purpose-built capital, Mansuriya. near Qairawan. Like Baghdad which was built by al-Mansur's Abbasid namesake, Mansuriya was circular in form, probably indicating his own pretensions to be ruler of the world. **In 969, in the wake of the conquest of Egypt, Muizz, the fourth Fatimid Caliph, transferred the capital to Cairo**. The economic prosperity and cultural vitality of Fatimid Cairo eclipsed that of Abbasid Baghdad. Al-Azhar, Cairo's principal mosque, which was built in 970, soon became a major centre of learning. It lays claim to being the oldest university in the world. From Egypt, the Fatimids extended into Palestine and Syria, and took over the guardianship of Mecca and Medina. For reasons which remain obscure, the sixth Caliph, al-Hakim (996–1021) destroyed the Church of the Holy Sepulchre. This was one of the factors which led ultimately to the launching of the First Crusade.

When Fatimid power was at its zenith, Persia and Iraq were controlled by another Shiite dynasty, the Buyids (also known as the Buwayids). They originated in Daylam, to the south-west of the Caspian Sea. Between 934 and 935 the three Buyid brothers Ali, Hasan and Ahmad, established themselves in Shiraz, Rayy and Baghdad respectively. Ahmad's son Adud-ad-Dawla, who reigned from 949 to 983, succeeded in uniting all the Buyid territories, which for a time even included Oman. After his death, however, the empire began to disintegrate.

Great Seljuks (1038–1194), Rum Seljuks (1077–1307) and Atabegs (1127–1270)

In the eleventh century, a Turkish people known as the **Seljuks** moved down from Central Asia and conquered Persia, gradually ousting the Buyids. The Abbasid Caliphs welcomed the invasion and regarded the Seljuks, who were staunch Sunnis, as the best hope for the revival of the caliphal empire. Therefore, **when their leader Toghril entered Baghdad in 1055, making it his capital, the Caliph confirmed him as Sultan**, the title which Toghril had assumed seventeen years earlier in Nishapur. In addition to putting pay to the Buyids, the Seljuks drove the Fatimids out of Syro-Palestine and the Arabian peninsula. Moreover, **in 1071 Seljuk forces defeated the Byzantine army at Manzikert and annexed practically the whole of Asia Minor**.

The Seljuk Turks were originally a nomadic people with no sense of national identity. Their primary loyalty was to their tribe and they were predisposed to view the Sultan as a Central Asian 'khan' who presided over a loose tribal confederacy. Nevertheless, the Sultans ruled in the tradition of Persian emperors establishing a bureaucracy, a standing army and tax collectors, and putting the government in the hands of a vizier (Arabic *wazir* 'minister of state') just as the Abbasid Caliphs had done. **A famous Seljuk vizier, the Persian Nizam al-Mulk, spearheaded the Sunni revival by founding and endowing** *madrasas* (Arabic 'places of learning') in all the major cities of the empire. These institutions fostered the study of the Hadith (the sayings of the Prophet) and Islamic law, and trained *ulama* (religious scholars). Two *madrasas*, the Nizamiya in Nishapur and its

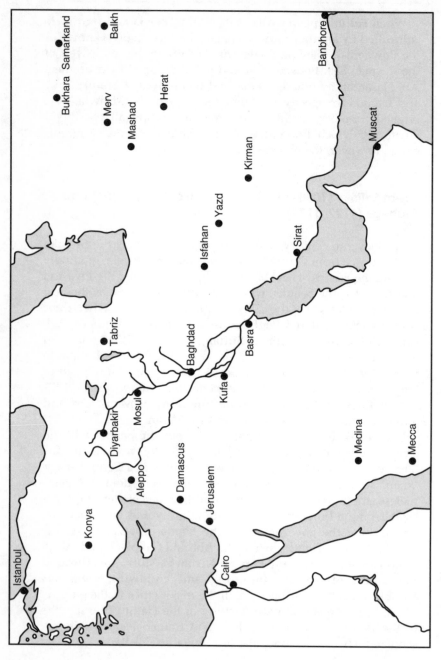

Figure 3 The Middle East and Central Asia

namesake in Baghdad, enjoyed a specially high reputation for scholarship.

Seljuk empire-building was hampered by two factors. In the first place, the Sultans were dependent on their nomadic subjects who guarded their frontiers, but these nomads frequently rebelled and invaded settled tax-paying areas. Secondly, in accordance with Central Asian custom, a Sultan's family expected to share his power during his lifetime and to divide his territorial possessions after his death. In the last quarter of the eleventh century, the empire began to fall apart. The Turks who had moved into Asia Minor formed a separate empire, that of the **Rum Seljuks**, and Seljuk princes established independent control of Syria. The Rum Seljuks took their name from *ar-Rum* (literally 'the Romans') the Quranic term for the Byzantines. Jalaluddin Rumi (d. 1273), the celebrated poet and mystic, lived in Konya, the Rum Seljuk capital. In 1095, fearing that the Rum Seljuks would cross the Bosphorus and take Constantinople itself, the Byzantine emperor Alexius I asked Pope Urban II for help. In response, Urban launched the First Crusade the following year. The Crusaders captured Nicaea in 1097, Edessa in 1098 and Jerusalem in 1099.

In the twelfth century, Seljuk control over Iraq was weakened by the political revival of the Abbasid caliphate. In Syro-Palestine the Seljuks had to cope with the Crusaders. Moreover, in the Arabian peninsula, Syria and Persia, the Seljuk sphere of influence was diminished by the rise of the **Atabegs** (= 'father commanders') who established local dynasties. The Atabegs were Turkish slave commanders who were originally sent out to act as guardians to the Seljuk princes who had been appointed provincial governors, but they seized the reins of power and ruled in their own name. The Atabegs were wiped out by the Mongol invasions of the mid-thirteenth century but the Rum Seljuks retained their independence for a further fifty years by paying the Mongols tribute.

The Mongols

Like the Seljuks, **the Mongols were originally nomadic tribes-men from Central Asia.** They appear to have haled from the Mongolian and Siberian forest fringes around Lake Baikal, but they entered history in the thirteenth century as fierce horsemen causing wholesale slaughter and destruction wherever they went. **In 1206 Chinggis (= Jenghis) Khan was proclaimed supreme chief of the Mongols. He rapidly created a vast empire incorporating most of Russia, China, Persia and Afghanistan.** Before his death in 1227, he divided his territories between his four sons. The details need not detain us; suffice it to note that the third son, Ögedey, succeeded his father as Great Khan. One of Ögedey's successor's, the Great Khan Mönke, entrusted his own brother Hülegü with the task of consolidating the Mongol hold on western Asia. **Hülegü sacked Baghdad in 1258** and ruled Persia, Iraq, the Caucasus and Anatolia as Il-Khan (subordinate of the Great Khan). Although the Mongols were originally pagans, the seventh Il-Khan, **Mahmud Ghazan (1295–1304), converted to Islam** and his successors were all Muslims. Chinggis Khan's eldest son, Jochi, died shortly before he did, but Jochi's descendants ruled over South Russia and Siberia as the Khans of the Golden Horde. Early in the fourteenth century, they too became Muslims. The Giray Khans who ruled the Crimea from 1426 to 1792 were descended from them. Chinggis's second son, Chaghatay, and his successors who ruled Transoxania and Turkestan, were far more resistant to Islam, although his distant descendants eventually helped to spread Islam in Chinese Turkestan, where they remained until the seventeenth century.

The Ayyubids (1169-c.1250) and Mamluks (1250–1517)

The **Ayyubids** were descended from Turkicised Kurdish warriors employed by the Seljuks in Syria. In 1169, one of these warriors conquered Egypt from the Fatimids but died almost immediately. His nephew Salah ad-Din, better known to Europeans as Saladin, established the dynasty. Salah ad-Din eradicated the influence of the Fatimids and promoted orthodox Sunnism. He also fought bravely against the Crusaders, recapturing Jerusalem in 1187. Before his death he divided his empire between various members of his family who established separate dynasties in the Yemen, Egypt, Damascus, Aleppo and Diyarbakr. The control of the Yemen was lost to the Rasulids in 1229; Egypt was conquered by the Mamluks in 1252; and

Damascus and Aleppo were sacked by the Mongols a few years later. By then, the Ayyubids were a spent force. Nevertheless, a local Ayyubid dynasty ruled Diyarbakr, in what is now southeast Turkey, until the last decades of the fifteenth century.

The **Mamluks** were originally mercenaries in the service of the Ayyubids. Their name is derived from the Arabic *mamluk*, which means a slave – literally 'one who is owned'. They were children imported from Turkish lands conquered by the Mongols and reared as an elite corps dedicated to the Sultans. At first they were fiercely loyal but **in 1250, following the death of the Ayyubid Sultan al-Malik as-Salih, they seized power in Egypt.** To preserve a semblance of continuity, they appointed al-Malik as-Salih's widow Shajar ad-Durr ('Tree of Pearls') as Sultan. She then married her Mamluk commander-in-chief, who promptly succeeded her. As upstarts with humble origins, the Mamluks needed somehow to give legitimacy to their regime. Their chance came when the Mongols sacked Baghdad in 1258. Although the Caliph, al-Mustasim, perished along with most of his family, his uncle al-Mustansir survived. **In 1261 the Mamluk Sultan, Baybars, installed al-Mustansir as Caliph in Cairo.** The Caliphs were now mere figureheads with no practical power but the Mamluks took care to preserve the Caliphal line.

The **Mamluks were famed for their military prowess. In 1260, they won a decisive victory over the Mongols at the Battle of Ayn Jalut** ('Goliath's Spring') in Palestine, causing them to retreat. The captured cities in Syria rose up against the Mongol garrisons, welcoming the victors and lynching Jews and Christians whom they suspected of collaboration with the enemy. The Mamluks subsequently seized the Ayyubid territories in Syria, and **by 1293 they had driven out the Crusaders.** They continued to rule in their own name up until 1516 when Egypt and Syria were annexed by the Ottomans. After this date they ruled on behalf of the Ottomans, and their leaders received the Turkish title *bey*, meaning 'governor'.

The Timurids 1370–1506

The Timurids are named after the Timur-i Lang ('Timur the Lame') better known in English as Tamerlane (d. 1405). He was

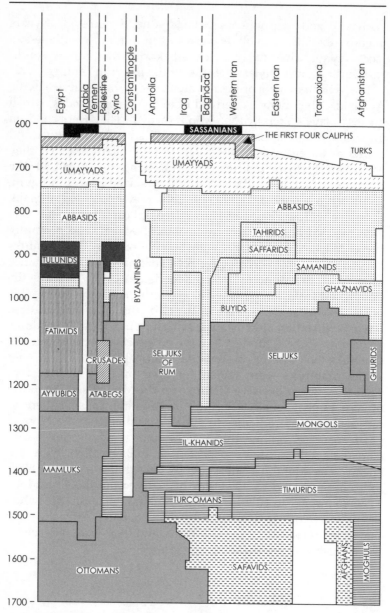

Figure 4 Chronological Chart Showing the Geographical Extent of the Principal Dynasties

born in Transoxania into a tribe of Mongol origin, which had become Turkish-speaking and had adopted Islam. The inscription on his tomb in Samarkand, which he made his capital, states that he was descended from Chinggis Khan. There is no substance to this claim although he did marry two Chinggizid princesses. Despite the fact that he was a Muslim, his barbarity matched that of the pagan Chinggis. Like him, he looted and burned the cities which he captured, having first slaughtered all their inhabitants. He even massacred Christians, not according them the protected status stipulated by Islamic law. He conquered Persia, Iraq and Georgia and sacked cities as far apart as Damascus and Delhi. Timur was not a constructive empire builder and gave little thought to what might happen to his domains after his death. In the event, there was civil war and his western territories were soon lost. His son Shah Rukh had greater respect for the Sharia than him and ruled Khurasan and Transoxania in relative peace. His unusual name, which means 'rook' or 'castle', was allegedly given him because Timur was playing chess when his birth was announced. Shah Rukh transferred the capital to Herat, which became a thriving centre of Timurid Islamic culture, especially during the long reign of Husayn Bayqara (1470–1506).

The Ottomans (1281–1924)

The Ottomans were Turkish tribesmen who were loosely attached to the Seljuk Sultans of Konya. In the thirteenth century with the appearance of the Mongols and the decline of the Seljuks, they were forced to migrate to north-western Anatolia. In 1326 they captured Bursa from the Byzantines and made it their capital. In 1357 they crossed into Europe at Gallipoli and rapidly overran a large part of the Balkans. In 1366 they transferred their capital to Edirne. After a serious setback caused by their defeat at the hands of the Mongols at the beginning of the fifteenth century, they reconstituted their empire and **Mehmet the Conqueror captured the Byzantine capital Constantinople in 1453**. The Ottomans pronounced its name as Istanbul. Its capture confirmed their status as an imperial power and it was destined to serve as their capital for the next 470 years.

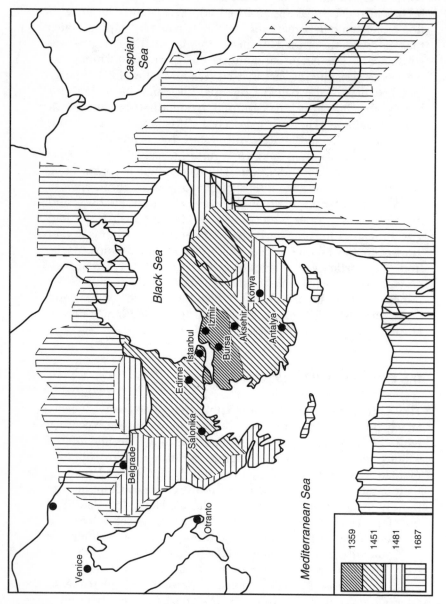

Figure 5 The Ottoman Empire

Caspian Sea

Black Sea

Mediterranean Sea

Venice
Otranto
Belgrade
Salonika
Edirne
Istanbul
Bursa
Izmir
Aksehir
Konya
Antalya

1359
1451
1481
1687

In the sixteenth century, the Ottomans entered their golden age. **In 1517, Selim the Grim conquered Egypt and Syria from the Mamlukes and brought the last Abbasid Caliph from Cairo to Istanbul.** After the Battle of Mohács in 1526, Suleyman the Magnificent (1520–1566) gained control of most of Hungary. During his long reign, he also subdued Iraq. Moreover, in North Africa, corsairs brought Libya, Tunisia and Algeria under Ottoman dominion.

In 1571, the Ottoman fleet was defeated in the Eastern Mediterranean by a European coalition at Lepanto. Although this marked the turning point in Ottoman fortunes, the Ottomans continued to pose a threat to Eastern Europe well into the second half of the seventeenth century, for as recently as 1683 they nearly succeeded in taking Vienna. The story of Ottoman decline in the eighteenth, nineteenth and early twentieth centuries, culminating in the abolition of the Caliphate in 1924, will be told in the next chapter.

The Safavids (1501–1732) and the Mughals (1526–1858)

At the beginning of the sixteenth century, when the Ottomans were entering their golden age, two other major dynasties were founded: the Safavids in Persia and the Mughals in North India. The **Safavids** were the descendants of Sheikh Safi ad-Din (d. 1334), who established the Safawiyya Sufi order at Ardabil in Azerbaijan. Although he was probably a Sunni, the order flourished in an area where Shiism was widespread and it consequently became openly Shiite during the fifteenth century. **In 1501, Shah Ismail I founded the Safavid dynasty in Persia and imposed Shiism as the state religion.** This gave Persia a distinct character, enabling it to resist incorporation into the Ottoman Empire and to survive down to the present day with its frontiers almost unchanged. The most famous Safavid monarch, Shah Abbas I (1588–1629), transformed Isfahan into one of the most splendid capitals in the world. After his death, the dynasty began to decline.

The **Mughals** came from Central Asia and were descendants of the Mongols, from whom they took their name. **The first Mughal emperor, Babur (1526–1530)** occupied Kabul in 1504, but it was not until 1526 that he conquered Delhi, which had Muslim rulers for the previous three hundred and twenty years. His son Humayun was forced to retreat to Afghanistan but finally established his hold on Delhi in 1555. Humayun's son **Akbar (1556–1605) conquered the whole of North India** creating an empire which extended from the Hindu Kush to the Bay of Bengal and from the Himalayas to the Arabian Sea. His successors pressed further south, expanding the empire to its greatest extent with the capture of Bijapur in 1686 and Golkonda in 1687.

Islam in the Horn of Africa, East Africa, Nubia, the Funj and South Africa

Some years before Muhammad emigrated to Medina, he encouraged a number of his followers to seek refuge in the Christian kingdom of Abyssinia. Thus, ever since the time of the Prophet, there has been an Islamic presence in Africa. By the eighth century, Muslim traders had gained control of the island of **Dahlak** off the coast of Ethiopia, and it became a thriving sultanate from the eleventh century to the middle of the thirteenth. By 900, the coastal strip from **Zaila to the tip of the Horn** had been Islamicised and Arab immigrants had established an Islamic state in the highlands of Eritrea which were known as the **Shoan Plateau**. By 1100, Islamic influence had extended down a narrow band of the **East African Coast** that included Mogadishu, Malindi, Mombassa, Zanzibar and Mozambique. Although Malindi was occupied by the Portuguese in 1493, and the other ports suffered the same fate in the first decade of the sixteenth century, the area continued to be predominantly Muslim. The last quarter of the fourteenth century saw the rise of the **Sultanate of Adal**. To begin with, this was confined to the coastal region around Zaila, and its hinterland, but under Ahmad Grañ, in the first half of the sixteenth century, it expanded to incorporate a large part of Abyssinia. When Ahmad Grañ died fighting the Portuguese, in 1543, his empire fell apart. From this point, although the influence of Muslims increased on the coast owing to Ottoman naval power, their influence in the interior declined and Islam was represented mainly by scattered groups of nomads without a central sultanate.

In the ninth century, Arab bedouin began to migrate to **Nubia** in increasing numbers, probably attracted by the gold mines south of Aswan. By the end of the tenth century, the bedouin had intermingled with the Nubians and Beja to produce an Arabic-speaking Muslim population of mixed blood. Around 1004, some of them established a principality in the region of Aswan, and were vassals of the Fatimids who gave them the name **Kanz ad-Dawla** ('Treasure of the State'). In the thirteenth and fourteenth centuries, Nubia was conquered by the Egyptian Mamluks, and in 1317 the cathedral of Dongola was converted into a mosque. With the Ottoman conquest of Egypt in 1517, Nilotic Sudan officially became part of the Ottoman Empire although in practice it continued to be ruled by the Mamluk beys. In the sixteenth century the **Funj**, who were of African origin, converted to Islam and established a nilotic kingdom further to the south.

The origins of Islam in **South Africa** are entirely different. The Dutch brought Malay, Javanese and Bengali Muslims and settled them around Cape Town in 1694. They are sometimes referred to as the Malay coloureds.

Islam in West Africa

From earliest times, merchants from Egypt and North Africa followed the caravan routes to West Africa where they could exchange their handicrafts and salt for gold and slaves. By the second half of the eleventh century, **Ghana** was ruled by Soninke Negroes and had a mixed population of animists and Muslims. The animists were persuaded to embrace Islam by the Almoravids and in due course the country came under the control of a Muslim Berber regime. By the thirteenth century, however, Ghana was conquered by the Susu, who were animists. The Muslims consequently fled further north and established a trading centre at Walata.

Mali was at one time a dependency of Ghana. However, under its first Muslim leader, Mansa Ulli (d. 1337), it became an empire extending from the Atlantic to Gao, bounded by Niani in the south, and by Walata and Awdaghust in the north.

Gao was the capital of the **Songhay** empire. From 1009, this was ruled by a Muslim dynasty called the Za, but not all their subjects embraced Islam. It was conquered by Mali in the fourteenth century and liberated by Sonni Ali in the fifteenth. Sonni Ali seized the flourishing trading centre of Timbuktu, which was also a major centre of Islamic scholarship. Songhay was eventually conquered by Morocco in 1591.

From the fourteenth century onwards, Muslims from Mali, the Volta and Songhay began to move into **Hausaland** but the conversion of this region was a slow and complex process. To the east of Hausaland, around Lake Chad, there grew up the empire of **Kanem-Borno**, which traded with Egypt and Tripoli. It was ruled by the Sayfawids from 1075 to 1808. Under King Idris Aloma (1570–1619) it was a major power in the central Sahara.

Islam in South-East Asia

Arab and Indian traders probably took Islam to south-east Asia hundreds of years before their presence there entered historical records. The first Muslim stronghold that we know of was **Pasai** on the northern tip of Sumatra, for the Malay Chronicle of Ajeh mentions a Muslim dynasty ruling the region from 1205 onwards. By 1500, Muslim traders had settled in many other areas and three Muslim empires had come into existence through the conversion of indigenous leaders. They were the Sultanates of **Malacca** (most of the Malay archipelago and part of the Sumatra coast), **Demak** (central Java, the southern tip of Borneo and south-east Sumatra) and **Ajeh** (north-west Sumatra). The late sixteenth and early seventeenth centuries saw the rise of the Sultanates of **Mataram** (most of Java, southern coast of Borneo and south-east Sumatra), **Macassar** (Celebes and the east coast of Borneo), **Bantam** (southern tip of Sumatra and northern tip of Java, including Jakarta) and **Brunei** (northern Borneo). Note that from the early sixteenth century onwards, the spread of Islam in the region was partly checked by the activities of the Portuguese, British, Spanish and Dutch. The Portuguese held Pasai from 1521 to 1524, and Malacca from 1511 to 1641; the British acquired Singapore in 1528; the Spanish occupation of the Philippines in 1570 penned the Muslims into the south of Mindanao, the most southerly of the islands; and in the course of the seventeenth century, the Dutch acquired extensive territories including most

of the Celebes, the coastal regions of the Malay Peninsula; and
the west coast of Sumatra.

Recapitulation: Four Successive Periods of Islamic History

At the beginning of this chapter, I mentioned six key events
beginning with the emigration to Medina in 622, and ending
with the defeat of the Turks at Lepanto in 1571. An alternative
way of structuring Islamic history, which might appeal to those
who have difficulty remembering precise dates, is to think of it as
comprising four successive eras of approximately 300 years, 350
years, 450 years and 300 years respectively: (1) c. 600–900 the
formative era; (2) c. 900–1250 the classical era; (3) c.1250–1700;
the post-classical era, (4) c. 1700 to the present, the modern era.
The first era takes us almost to the time when the Fatimid
dynasty was founded. The reason for labelling it 'formative' will
become clear in subsequent chapters when we examine the
development of Shiism and the Sunni law schools. The second
era ends with the Mongol invasions and the loss of most of
Spain. The reason for locating the end of the third era and the
beginning of the fourth around 1700 will be explained in the next
chapter, when we broach the subject of Islam in the modern
world.

4 Islam in the modern world

Introduction

The modern era of Islamic history may be divided into **FOUR PERIODS**. The precise point at which one period ends and another begins is debatable. It might, therefore, be better to think of them as four overlapping phases. Nevertheless, the following scheme, although undoubtedly oversimplified, has the advantage that it is relatively easy to remember. **The first period, 1699–1798, was a century of decline and reform**. The decline of the three great Muslim empires arguably began several decades before this. Nevertheless, I have taken 1699 as the symbolic beginning because in that year, as a result of the Treaty of Karlowitz, the Ottoman Empire lost extensive territories for the first time. **The second period, 1798–1922, was characterised by European domination**. European domination of the Muslim heartland began with Napoleon's expedition to Egypt in 1798, and reached its greatest geographical extent when the League of Nations (the forerunner of the United Nations) gave France and Britain mandates to rule the newly-created Arab states in 1920. **The third period, 1922–1962, was one of decolonialisation and the origins of Islamism**. Because Egypt gained limited independence in 1922, I have taken that date as marking the beginning of the period. The following year saw the birth of the Republic of Turkey, the first modern Muslim nation state, which rose from the ashes of the dismembered Ottoman empire. However, most Muslim countries gained their independence much later, the majority of them between 1945 and 1960. Although the dominant ideology during this period was nationalism, some Muslims founded religio-political parties with a view to establishing a truly Islamic state. This type of politicised Islam is often misleadingly called 'Islamic fundamentalism'. The more technical term for it is 'Islamism'. **The fourth period, 1962 to the present, has been characterised by Islamic resurgence**. It began in 1962, with the founding of the Meccan-based World Muslim League, an international organisation geared to propagating the faith. Islamic revival did not, however, gain momentum until the late sixties, by which time many Muslims had become disillusioned with nationalism and other western ideologies. A watershed was reached in 1979 when Ayatollah Khomeini led an Islamic revolution in Iran.

1699–1798 Decline & Reform: (a) The Decline of the Three Great Muslim Empires

By the end of the seventeenth century, **the Ottoman Empire** had begun to decline. At the Treaty of Carlowitz in 1699, the Ottomans were forced to surrender Hungary and Transylvania to Austria, and the Ukraine to Poland, thereby reversing their previous policy of expansion. In the course of the eighteenth century, the situation continued to deteriorate: Turkish ports were flooded with European manufactured goods; the imperial finances were mishandled; there was lack of discipline amongst the janissaries, the elite corps of the infantry; and the Muslim world seemed generally to be losing its vitality. The Ottoman Sultans attempted to rally the Muslim subjects of their far-flung territories, as well as Muslims outside the empire, by styling themselves Caliph. They first used this title in the Russo-Ottoman Treaty of 1774, despite subsequent claims that the Caliphate had been transferred to them officially by the last Abbasid in 1517.

The Safavid Empire fared even worse. After the death of Shah Abbas II in 1666, the Persian throne was occupied by a series of drunkards who drained the treasury by their opulent lifestyle. In the early years of the eighteenth century, the governor of Afghanistan declared himself independent, and in 1722, his son, Mahmud of Qandahar, invaded Persia and captured Isfahan. Within a few years, the Afghans were ousted by a tribal chieftain called Nadir, whom Shah Tahmasp II rewarded with the governorship of Khurasan, Sistan, Kirman and Mazandaran. Having driven out the Afghans, Nadir turned on Persia's external enemies, Turkey and Russia. When the Shah concluded a treaty with them, Nadir dethroned him, at first setting up another Safavid as a puppet ruler and then having himself proclaimed Nadir Shah in 1736. Two years later, he led the most successful of all his campaigns, invading India and exacting tribute from the Mughal Emperor. The revival of Persia's fortunes under Nadir Shah did not last. With his assassination in 1747, the country was plunged into chaos and various military leaders seized power in the provinces: Nadir Shah's dynasty, the Afsharids, retained control of Khurasan whilst the Zands and Qajars competed for the remaining territory. Persia was eventually reunified by the Qajar ruler, Shah Agha Muhammad, in 1794.

The Mughal Empire also began to decline in the latter half of the seventeenth century, but for different reasons. The Mughals had extended their influence in India by leaving the socio-religious fabric of the indigenous Hindu society virtually intact. However, the Emperor Awrangzib (1658–1707) abandoned this policy and adopted one of Islamicisation. This led to widespread revolt throughout his domains. The most serious opposition came from the Marathas who carved out their own state in the Deccan. Although Awrangzib drove them south, thereby expanding his territory still further, he was unable to crush them. After his death, the empire began to disintegrate: no less than ten emperors succeeded him in the space of twelve years; Delhi was sacked by Nadir Shah of Iran in 1738–9, and again by Ahmad Shah Abdali of Afghanistan in 1756–7; the Marathas seized Gujurat in 1750 and rapidly extended their control eastwards; Oudh became a separate Shiite principality in 1754; by 1757 the British, who had been trading in India for over half a century, had come to dominate Bengal; and in 1799 the Sikhs, who had been savagely repressed by Awrangzib and had suffered a series of Afghan invasions, finally gained control of the Punjab.

1699–1798 Decline and Reform: (b) Early Attempts at Reform

While the power of the three great Muslim empires was waning, there emerged throughout the Muslim world a number of reformers who preached what they considered to be a return to a purer more rigorous Islam. They differed considerably, not least in their attitude to Sufism, some regarding it as an aberration but others using it as a vehicle for spreading their teaching. What most of them had in common, however, was a renewed emphasis on the Quran and Hadith as sources of guidance; a recognition of the importance of *ijtihad* (the exercise of independent judgement in questions of law); a rejection of many of the accretions of medieval Islam; and a critical attitude to the Muslim rulers of their day. Four such reformers will be mentioned here, although there were many others. **Muhammad Baqir Majlisi (1628–1700) was the leading reformer in Safavid Persia.** He is mentioned in this context for that reason, despite the fact that he died right at the beginning of the period. He compiled a massive collection of Shiite traditions known as *Bihar al-Anwar* (The Ocean of Lights); attempted to suppress Islamic philosophy, Sufism and Sunni Islam throughout the realm; and argued that the *mujtahids* (the senior religious scholars who were qualified to practise *ijtihad*) were the legitimate rulers of the Shiite state. The Sunni scholar **Shah Wali Allah of Delhi (1703–62) played a not dissimilar role in Mughal India.** He revived the study of the Hadith; propagated a reformed Naqshbandi Sufism, shorn of popular superstitions; and founded a school of thought which continues to influence religious thought in Muslim India. Whereas the majority of Sunni scholars, unlike their Shiite counterparts, held that 'the door of *ijtihad*' had been closed since the tenth century, and that jurists were therefore bound to follow earlier precedents, Wali Allah appealed to the writings of the Syrian jurist Ibn Taymiya (1263–1328) in support of his claim that *ijtihad* was still permissible. **Within the Ottoman Empire, a more radical position was espoused by the Arab reformer Muhammad ibn Abd al-Wahhab (1703–92).** He regarded the Quran and the Hadith as the only sources of law; was an intrepid opponent of all aspects of Sufism and popular religion including reverence for the Prophet's tomb in Medina; and favoured armed revolt against the Ottomans. In 1744, he allied himself with Ibn Saud, the head of minor tribal dynasty in central Arabia. From then on, the influence of the Wahhabis steadily spread through central and western Arabia. **Finally, in West Africa, Shehu Usuman dan Fodio (1754–1817) launched reforms which led to the creation of the Sultanate of Sokoto.** He was a learned scholar and Sufi, with a wide-ranging knowledge of classical Islamic texts and was haled by his followers as the *mujaddid*, or 'Renewer', of the thirteenth century of the Islamic era, which began on November 4th 1785. He waged *jihad* in Hausaland between 1804 and 1810; imposed the Sharia; and established an Islamic government modelled on the classical Caliphate to replace the Hausa kings whose syncretistic Islam he regarded as little better than paganism.

1798–1922 European Domination: (a) The Demise of the Ottoman Empire

From 1798 to 1801, Napoleon Bonaparte occupied **Egypt**. Although the occupation was short-lived, it was of great significance because it was the first occasion since the Crusades that a European power had gained control of any part of the Muslim heartland. Moreover, the French initiated administrative reforms which set Egypt on the path of modernisation. The departure of Napoleon's troops left a power vacuum, which was filled when Muhammad Ali seized power in 1805 and was recognised as Viceroy by Istanbul. By this time, the Wahhabis had begun to pose a serious threat to Ottoman authority: they had invaded southern Iraq, and had also occupied Mecca and Medina, the two holy cities of Arabia. Eventually, in 1811, the Ottoman Sultan called on Muhammad Ali to send troops to crush the rebellion. This strengthened Muhammad Ali's position, enabling him to become virtually the independent ruler of Egypt. He massacred the Mamluks and modernised Egypt's administrative, economic and military organisation on European lines. In 1831, he rebelled against the Ottomans and annexed Syria. He was forced to relinquish it in 1840 but was then recognised as the hereditary ruler of Egypt. His grandson, the Khedive Ismail, who ruled from 1863 to 1869, was an even more enthusiastic moderniser than him. His vast expenditure on railways, the Suez canal and the Cairo Opera House, brought the country to the brink of bankruptcy and forced it to accept Franco-British financial control. In 1882, Britain intervened to quell a nationalist uprising, and two years later appointed a Consul General who was the ruler of Egypt in all but name.

Muhammad Ali and the Wahhabis were not the only military threats to the Ottoman Empire. It would take too long to chronicle its disintegration in detail. Suffice it to note that **Greece** gained independence in 1829; **Serbia** became fully autonomous in 1830; the French conquered **Algeria** between 1830 and 1847; **Bulgaria** came into existence in 1878; Austria seized **Bosnia** and **Herzegovina** the same year; **Tunisia** was made a French protectorate in 1881; Italy conquered **Libya** in 1911–12; and most of the remaining **European territories** were lost in the Balkan Wars of 1912–13.

Throughout the nineteenth century, the Ottomans had also repeatedly suffered the hostility of the Russians. The Russians had been their bitter enemies in the Russo-Turkish Wars of 1829–30 and 1877–78, and the Crimean War of 1853–56. Britain, on the other hand, had generally supported the Ottomans diplomatically and had fought alongside them in the Crimea. In 1907, however, fearing the rising power of Germany, she entered into the Anglo-Russian Entente. In 1914, when war broke out between Germany and the triple alliance Britain-France-Russia, the Ottomans at first chose to remain neutral. Nevertheless, fear of the likely effects of a Russian victory eventually led them to side with Germany. The Ottoman Sultan, in his capacity as Caliph, called on all Muslims to engage in *jihad* against Britain and her allies. Britain reacted by declaring Egypt a protectorate and deposing the pro-Ottoman Khedive. She also curried the favour of the Sultan's disaffected Arab subjects, including the Sharif of Mecca, giving them assurance that Britain was prepared to recognise and support Arab independence. In the event, this independence, which was won in the course of the war, proved to be severely circumscribed by British interests. For unknown to the Arabs, in 1916 Britain and France were signatories to the Sykes-Picot Agreement, which laid detailed plans for dividing the post-Ottoman Middle East into British and French spheres of influence. In the aftermath of the war, the Sharif of Mecca became King Hussein of **the Hejaz**, and five new and largely artificial

Arab states – Jordan, Iraq, Palestine, Syria and Lebanon – were created out of other former Ottoman territories. Hussein's two sons became the kings of **Jordan** and **Iraq**, but under British tutelage; **Palestine** was ruled directly by British mandate, and **Syria** and **Lebanon** by French mandate. Mustafa Kemal (later known as Atatürk – 'Father Turk') moulded what was left of the Ottoman Empire into the modern secular state of **Turkey**.

1798–1922 European Domination: (b) the Colonisation of the Muslim World

Between 1798, when Napoleon set foot in Egypt, and 1920, when the French and British received the mandates for the newly created Arab states, practically the whole of the Muslim world came under European influence. We have dealt with the dismemberment of the Ottoman Empire but must now briefly chronicle the European colonisation of the Muslim lands which lay beyond the Ottoman frontiers.

The **Dutch** government took over from the Dutch East Indian Company in 1800 and completed the colonisation of the Indonesian archipelago by 1908. The **British** achieved hegemony over India in 1818; established protectorates in the Malay states between 1874 and 1914; established an Anglo-Egyptian condominion over the Sudan in 1898; and absorbed most of the Sultanate of Sokoto into Northern Nigeria, where they established a protectorate in 1900. **Russia** extended her territories in Central Asia, between 1854 and 1895, by annexing the lands of the Kazakhs, the Khanate of Khokand, the lands of the Turkomans and Tajiks, and the ancient Khanates of Khiva and Bukhara. The **French**, who had established a trading post in Senegal as long ago as 1637, colonised French West Africa between the early 1880s and 1912, the year in which they also made Morocco a protectorate.

The effect which incorporation in European empires had on Muslim countries was not uniform. The French, for example, attempted to make Algeria part of France, encouraging mass immigration of colonists but only offering French citizenship to Algerians who were prepared to relinquish the Sharia. Elsewhere, their approach was more moderate, especially in those countries where they only established protectorates. The British, on the other hand, generally avoided interfering in the religious affairs of their subjects except when they posed a threat to security. In India they encouraged Muslims to be Muslims and Hindus to be Hindus, on the principle of divide and rule; and in Northern Nigeria the Sharia was enforced more rigorously by them than it had been by the Sultans of Sokoto, although the prescribed punishments for theft and adultery were not implemented. Nevertheless, despite these differences, European imperialism was almost invariably divisive because it produced a Europeanised social elite. Modern cities grew up alongside ancient walled *madinas*; modern European-style schools and colleges vied with traditional Islamic *madrasas*; dual systems of administration were introduced; and Christian missionaries sought to make converts.

1798–1922 European Domination: (c) Muslim Responses to Colonialisation

The reactions of Muslim scholars and religious leaders to European domination varied considerably. The only notable attempt at orchestrating a pan-Islamic response was made by **Jalal ad-Din al-Afghani** (1839–97). Despite his name he was almost certainly not an Afghan but an Iranian. He visited Egypt, India and Istanbul preaching against European imperialism and encouraging Muslims everywhere to rally behind the Ottoman Sultan in the face of European aggression, even hoping to persuade the Shah to acknowledge the Sultan as Caliph if the Sultan gave him control of the Shiite holy cities in Iraq. The modernising process which the French inaugurated in Egypt led to the opening of the first Arab printing press in 1822, which in turn made possible an Arab renaissance. One of the leading figures of this renaissance was al-Afghani's pupil and admirer **Muhammad Abduh** (1849–1905). He rose to be Chief Mufti of Egypt but despite his training as a religious scholar he wrote in a style which was accessible to Arabs who had had a Western-style education. He argued that the Muslim world had been overrun by Europeans, not because there was anything intrinsically wrong or inadequate about Islam but because the majority of Muslims were bad Muslims. He was an indefatigable opponent of *taqlid*, the uncritical acceptance of legal precedents, and suggested that those who advocated it were little better than the Meccan pagans who had adhered stubbornly to their ancestral traditions and rejected the message of Islam. He called for a return to sources, notably the Quran, the Sunna (practice of the Prophet) as enshrined in the hadiths, and the beliefs and practices of 'the pious forefathers' (*as-salaf as-salih*). The reform movement which he inspired came to be known as the Salafiya. It had a considerable influence on Ibn Badis, the leading Muslim reformer in French Algeria, and on the Muhammadiyya movement in Dutch Indonesia. In India, the principal resistance to British influence came from the reformist tradition of Shah Wali Allah. In 1867, two scholars from this tradition, **Muhammad Qasim Nanautawi** and **Rashid Ahmad Gangohi**, founded the seminary at Deoband which subsequently spawned daughter institutions throughout the subcontinent. Indian modernists were a minority. Their champion was **Sayyid Ahmad Khan** (1817–98). He was passionately pro-British and established the Anglo-Oriental College at Aligarh in 1877, so that Muslims could benefit from a western-style education. His radical views will be mentioned in the course of the next chapter. In the first half of the twentieth century, Muslims were divided in their political aspirations. Some backed the National Congress's demand for self-government whereas others, like **Muhammad Iqbal** (1876–1938) the distinguished lawyer and poet, could see no future in co-operating with the Hindu majority and pressed instead for the establishment of Pakistan as a homeland for Muslims.

1798–1922 European Domination: (d) the European Impact on Turkey and Iran

Ottoman Turkey, Qajar Iran, North Yemen, Afghanistan and central Arabia were the only significant Muslim territories to escape direct European domination. Nevertheless, two of these, Turkey and Iran, were profoundly influenced by Europe in a less direct manner.

In **Turkey**, during the heyday of the Ottoman Empire, the *ulama* had a virtual monopoly of the administration of justice, the staffing of educational establishments, and the control of charitable trusts.

From 1838 onwards, however, all this began to change as the Ottoman Sultans introduced a series of sweeping reforms incorporating elements of European law into the legislative system and founding European-style schools and academies. In 1923, the Republic of Turkey was born. The following year Mustafa Kemal abolished the Caliphate, religious schools and religious courts. He subsequently introduced a new law code based on that of the Swiss; suppressed the Sufi *tariqas*; and substituted the Latin alphabet for the time-honoured Arabic script.

The situation in **Iran** was somewhat different. At the beginning of the nineteenth century, the country, although formally reunified by the Qajars, was in reality a collection of semi-autonomous states in some of which a high proportion of the population were tribesmen. Because of the weakness of the central government, it was relatively easy for the European powers to make inroads. Russia, as Iran's northern neighbour was well-situated to annex the most northerly territories including Azerbayjan and to have an influence on the northern half of the country. Britain, however, was concerned to keep Russia away from the Persian Gulf and India, and therefore exerted continual pressure on the southern half. The commercial rivalry between Russian and Britain was intense and several of the Shahs proved unpopular with their subjects for granting them commercial monopolies in railway construction, banking, mining and petroleum extraction. The Shiite *ulama*, on the contrary, consolidated their power by championing resistance to European interference. For instance, in 1890 a British consortium was granted a monopoly of tobacco but the following year the supreme Shiite jurist issued a *fatwa* declaring the use of tobacco unlawful. This was universally obeyed and the concession became worthless. In the twentieth century, however, the country became increasingly secular. After Reza Shah ascended the throne in 1925, he curtailed the power of the *ulama*, outlawed the veiling of women, and forced men to wear western dress.

1922–1962 Decolonialisation and the Origins of Islamism

Britain recognised Egypt as an independent country in 1922, but she retained considerable influence there until the Free Officers' revolution thirty years later, and evacuated the Suez Canal Zone only in 1954. In 1924, the Wahhabis, who controlled central Arabia, invaded the Hejaz and evicted King Hussein. Their leader, Abd al-Aziz ibn Saud, assumed the title King of the Hejaz and Najd in 1926, renaming his country Saudi Arabia after six years. Iraq gained independence in 1932; Lebanon in 1941. In the wake of the Second World War, the process of decolonialisation continued apace. Syria became independent in 1945, Jordan in 1946; Pakistan was created in 1947, and Indonesia in 1949; Libya drove out the Italians in 1951; Morocco, Sudan and Tunisia gained their freedom in 1956; Malaya came into existence in 1957, Mauritania, Mali, Niger, Nigeria, Upper Volta and Somalia in 1960. The French were reluctant to abandon Algeria but did so eventually in 1962 after an eight-year struggle. By this time, Muslims almost everywhere, with the exception of those in the Soviet Union, had shaken off the colonial yoke. However, there was one event which ran counter to the decolonialisation of the Muslim world: the state of **Israel was established on Palestinian soil in 1948** and Jews began flocking there, many of them to escape persecution.

The creation of Israel came as no surprise to Muslims, because in 1917 the British government had issued the Balfour Declaration announcing that it favoured the establishing in Palestine of a national home for the Jewish people. **In 1928, Hasan al-Banna (1906–49), an Egyptian school teacher living in the Suez Canal Zone, founded the *Ikhwan al-Muslimin* (Muslim Brotherhood)** as a youth group stressing moral and spiritual reform. The movement gained in popularity as a result of growing ant-British feeling caused by Zionist activity in Palestine, and **in 1939 it became a political party with the avowed aim of liberating Egypt and the rest of the Muslim world from alien control and establishing a genuinely Islamic government.** Members of the *Ikhwan* blamed the Egyptian authorities for Israel's victory over the Arabs in 1948. As a result of this, the movement was swiftly outlawed. One of its members assassinated the Prime Minister and the following year, security agents killed al-Banna in retaliation. In 1950, however, the *Ikhwan* was legalised again and its members assisted in the 1952 coup which overthrew King Farouk. The new military rulers imposed martial law but exempted the *Ikhwan* from the ban on political parties on the grounds that it was a religious organisation. Nevertheless, this uneasy alliance did not last long, for in 1954 there was an abortive attempt at assassinating Colonel Nasser. This led to the execution of four activists, the imprisonment of 4,000 others and the voluntary exile of many more.

In 1941, a similar movement, *Jamaat-i Islami* (the Islamic Party), was founded in India by Abu 'l-Ala Mawdudi (1903–79), who subsequently moved to Pakistan. The *Ikhwan* and the *Jamaat* both conceive of Islam as an all-embracing religio-political system which is totally incompatible with all secular ideologies. Nevertheless, both advocate the use of science and technology, which they consider to be value-free; both appeal to the western-educated city-dwelling lower middle classes; and both dismiss the majority of the traditionalist *ulama* as obscurantist and hopelessly compromised with the status quo.

In 1952, a third religio-political party, *Hizb at-Tahrir* (the Liberation Party), was founded in Jordan by Taqi ad-Din an-Nabhani (1909–77) but has remained outlawed there. Although Nabhani lived in a Muslim country which had recently gained its independence, he regarded all the Arab heads of state as puppets who were manipulated by the colonial powers, and he held that Israel had been established by the West to perpetuate an imperialist presence in the heart of the Muslim world. His party worked towards the replacement of all the Muslim nation-states with a single Islamic government and the re-establishment of the Caliphate. It would be the duty of the Caliph, once elected, to lead a *jihad* against the unbelievers and liberate the whole of Palestine from the Israelis.

1962 to the Present: (a) Reasons for Islamic Resurgence

In Muslim countries struggling to shake off the yoke of European colonialism, Islam was not simply a religion, it was a rallying cry. Nevertheless, as an impetus for decolonialisation, Islam was generally subservient to nationalism. Moreover in most instances, those who steered their people through the transition from colonial rule to independence were neither traditionalist *ulama* nor Islamists; they were members of the westernised elite. This suited the erstwhile colonial powers because it made it easier for them to retain a significant degree of control over the Muslim world through economic aid and industrial, agricultural and educational projects. In the early years of independence, the nationalist leaders were heroes who could do no wrong in the eyes of the masses, even when they advocated or enacted policies which might in retrospect be perceived as anti-Islamic. For example, President Bourguiba of Tunisia urged his people not to observe the fast of Ramadan, on the grounds that doing so would damage the economy, and he closed the Zitouna thereby putting an end to twelve centuries of Islamic higher education in his country. During the nineteen-sixties, however, the tide began to turn and many Muslims started to look to their religious roots and advocate the reaffirmation of Islamic values. The reasons for this are highly complex. The following factors were involved but the list is not intended to be exhaustive

1 The enormous revenues from the sale of petroleum oil enabled Muslims in Saudi Arabia and the Gulf States to finance Islamic mission (Arabic *dawa* 'call', 'invitation') throughout the world. This was done through the distribution of literature as well as through donations to Muslim organisations channelled discreetly through local branches of the World Islamic League which was founded in 1962.

2 Many ordinary Muslims became disillusioned with the 'progressive' forces of nationalism and socialism. It fast became apparent that the western-educated secularised elites, who governed their countries, were unlikely to bring the benefits of modernity to the population at large. In many countries this increasing disillusionment was exacerbated by chronic unemployment, especially amongst the youth who comprised the majority of the population.

3 The 1967 Six-Day War resulted in Egypt's humiliating defeat and Israel's occupation of the Sinai Peninsula, the Gaza Strip, the West Bank and the Golan Heights. UN resolution 242 calling for her withdrawal from these territories was not enforced. This convinced the Muslim masses that Europe and the United States would invariably side with Israel. Their suspicions were confirmed by the Congress's support for Israel in the October War of 1973 and by western non-

intervention when Israel bombed Palestinian bases in the Lebanon in 1982. All three events produced widespread disenchantment with the West and western values.

4 The Arab oil-producing countries were enraged by the scale of Congress's military support for Israel in 1973 and reacted by imposing an oil embargo on Europe and the USA. The ensuing dramatic rise in the cost of petroleum caused serious inflation in Europe so that several European governments panicked and passed draconian immigration laws. This convinced Muslims who had come to Europe as migrant workers in the nineteen-fifties and sixties, that they were there to stay. In the mid-seventies, they therefore began to build mosques and Islamic cultural centres, assisted by donations from Muslims in the countries which had imposed the embargo!

5 In 1977, General Zia ul-Haq came to power in Pakistan as a result of a bloodless military coup. He imposed martial law and in 1979 he ordered the execution of his predecessor, President Zulfikar Ali Bhutto. Zia sought to win the support of both the traditionalist *ulama* and the Islamists by agreeing to Islamicise Pakistan's legal system.

6 In February 1979, the exiled Ayatollah Khomeini returned to Iran to lead the revolution which toppled the Shah and established what many Muslims hailed as the first genuinely Islamic state in the post-colonial period. Despite the deep-seated differences between Sunnism and Shiism, Khomeini succeeded in presenting his particular brand of revolutionary Islam as a product for export.

7 The fifteenth century of the Islamic era began on November 21, 1979. On the basis of a *hadith*, Sunni and Shiite Muslims expect the turn of every century to be a time of revival. Many of them looked upon Khomeini as the latest of a series of divinely-sent *mujaddids* ('renewers') of the faith.

8 Russia invaded Afghanistan in December 1979. This brought about a change in the US attitude to Pakistan. Whereas President Zia was previously regarded as an international pariah, he now became a hero in the fight against communism. The US and Saudi Arabia used Pakistan as a channel through which to pour funds into Afghanistan in support of the Mujahidin. The funds were transmitted via Pakistani

Islamists who acted as middlemen and who creamed off part of them to finance their own operations.

9 In September 1988, Salman Rushdie published *The Satanic Verses*. The novel is highly offensive to Muslims because it contains crude and defamatory allusions to the rise of Islam. For example, one of Rushdie's character's, a charlatan who invents a new religion, is called Mahound, a name given to Muhammad in medieval Christian literature; and another character, a prostitute called Ayesha, has the same name as the Prophet's favourite wife. Nevertheless, the furore over the book also owed much to the prevailing political circumstances at the time of its publication. A month before it was published, President Zia ul-Haq and five of his generals died in an air crash. In the ensuing elections, Pakistan's Islamists were routed and, on December 1, Zulfikar Ali Bhutto's daughter Benazir was sworn in as Prime Minister. It is no coincidence that the first anti-Rushdie demonstrations occurred shortly after this in Karachi, where the novelist had relatives. The demonstrations were orchestrated by Benazir Bhutto's Islamist opponents who wished to tar her with the same brush as him, on the grounds that she had had a similar western education. Meanwhile in Iran, Khomeini's reputation had been seriously dented by his acceptance of the ceasefire which put an end to the bloody eight-year conflict with Iraq, a war which he had vowed to win no matter how great the cost. His already bruised ego suffered a further blow when Rushdie depicted him in the novel as the turbaned Imam with eyes as white as clouds, whose megalomania led him to suppose that the death of his country's youth in battle was proof of their love for him (see especially pp. 205–15). Thus Khomeini had ulterior motives for pronouncing the notorious *fatwa* against Rushdie in February 1989: he wished both to regain his position as the foremost international spokesman of the Islamic resurgence and to wreak his revenge on the man who had satirised him.

10 In August 1990, Iraq invaded Kuwait. Twelve members of the Arab League resolved to back UN sanctions and to send troops to help the USA defend Saudi Arabia. The remaining eight members – the PLO, Jordan, Algeria, Tunisia, Yemen, Sudan, Libya and Mauritania – were opposed to American

intervention. Moreover, as soon as the bombardment of Baghdad began in January 1991, there was a groundswell of popular support for Iraq in a number of countries like Morocco which had voted for the resolution. This had little to do with Saddam Hussein's personality, despite his attempt to play the Islamic card. What shocked ordinary Muslims almost everywhere was the sight of the most powerful nation on earth crushing the people of a third-world country in defence of two mega-rich oil states in which almost all the wealth was concentrated in the hands of the ruling families.

1962 to the Present: (b) Radical Islamism

The *Ikhwan al-Muslimin*, the oldest of the Islamist movements, embraces a wide spectrum of opinions. Many of its current members in Egypt are moderates who seek to create an Islamic state by democratic means. Nevertheless, as we have seen, as early as 1948 its ranks included militants who were prepared to carry out assassinations. Nasser's suppression of the *Ikhwan* in 1954 led to its increasing radicalisation. The movement's leading ideologue, Sayyid Qutb (1906–66), was among those who were imprisoned and tortured. He considered that Nasser's Egypt was no better than Arabia during the *Jahiliya*, the period of ignorance which preceded the rise of Islam, and he acquiesced with those who inferred from this that it was permissible to engage in *jihad* against the government. He was hanged in 1966, after being implicated in a failed attempt to assassinate the President. Apart from a brief interlude in 1964, the *Ikhwan* was outlawed in Egypt between 1954 and 1975. In that year, Nasser's successor Anwar Sadat granted its members an amnesty, and in 1976 fifteen of them were elected to Parliament either as independents or as representatives of the ruling party. Sadat's success in co-opting the *Ikwan* into the political establishment led to the formation of militant splinter groups including *at-Takfir wa l-Hijra* ('The Denunciation and Migration') and *Munazzamat al-Jihad* ('The Jihad Organization'). In 1981, after armed clashes between Muslims and Christians, Sadat ordered the arrest of 1,500 people, dismissed Pope Shenouda the head of the Coptic Church, dissolved 15 religious organisations and banned the

Ikhwan. A month later, four members of *Munazzamat al-Jihad* gunned him down.

It would take too long to unravel the history of the sister branches of the Egyptian *Ikhwan* which exist in other Arab countries, or to assess the connections between Pakistan's *Jamaat-i Islami,* which fields parliamentary candidates, other Islamist groups in Pakistan, and the *Taliban,* who are currently taking over Afghanistan. Nor is there time to chronicle the development of the Islamic Salvation Front and other Islamist groups in Algeria. Mention must, however, be made of the Shiite *Hizb-Allah* ('God's Party'). Its alleged founder was Ayatollah Mahmoud Ghaffari who was imprisoned and tortured to death under the Shah. When he died in Qom in 1973 his last words were, 'There is only one party, God's Party' (cp. *Quran* 5.56, 58.22). However, there was no significant movement of this name until the Iranian Revolution of 1979, when Ghaffari's son emerged as the leader of a mob of ruffians who attacked enemies of the new regime on the streets of Iran. In 1982, Khomeini ordered the various Shiite terrorist groups to amalgamate with *Hizb-Allah,* and henceforth even the ruling Islamic Republic Party was viewed merely as one of its branches. Nevertheless, although *Hizb-Allah* has training camps in Iran for freedom-fighters who are active in the Lebanon and other parts of the world, it is a loose network rather than a tight-knit organisation like the Sunni Islamist movements.

1962 to the Present: (c) Islam versus Islamism?

In the course of the twentieth century, there have been two important developments which have affected Muslims everywhere: the emergence of Muslim nation-states and the birth of Islamist movements. Nationalist sentiments are not of course new to Muslims. The Umayyad Empire, for example, was in a sense the product of Arab nationalism, as its dissatisfied non-Arab citizens were acutely aware. Nevertheless, the boundaries of the modern Muslim nation-states, their forms of government, and their legal systems, are to a large extent the legacy of European colonialism. Similarly the Islamist movements, although they claim to be modelled on the life of the Prophet and the authentic Islam of the pre-Umayyad period, in fact owe a great deal to extraneous influences. Admittedly, like Muhammad's Meccan Companions, the Islamists are conscious of belonging to a minority at odds with the society in which they live. Like them, they are often prepared to migrate to places where their message may prove more acceptable. (When the Muslim Brotherhood was banned in Egypt in 1948 and again in 1954, hundreds of activists moved to other Arab states; when India was partitioned in 1947, Mawdudi and the majority of his followers migrated to Pakistan). Finally, like them too, their ultimate aim is to establish a theocratic state based on the Quran. There, however, the similarities end. In structure and leadership style, the Islamist movements bear a closer resemblance to European Fascist parties and Marxist-Leninist organisations than to the movement founded by Muhammad. Moreover, they could not function without the printed word, not to mention audio-cassettes and videos.

It is only by recognising that Muslim nation-states and Islamist movements are both comparatively recent developments that one may avoid the error of supposing that the former represent authentic Islam whereas the latter are a modern fundamentalist perversion of it. Throughout history there have been Muslims who have used Islam to establish their power and influence, as well as Muslims who have used their power and influence to establish Islam. The twentieth century is no exception and neither the Muslim nation-states nor the Islamist movements have a monopoly of one type of leadership. There are devout Muslim politicians who believe sincerely that modern western-style government best serves the interests of their fellow countrymen and of Islam, and there are others who pay lipservice to Islam in order to manipulate the masses. The same is true *mutatis mutandis* of those who hold the key positions in Islamist movements.

Recognising that there are politicians and activists who masquerade as Muslims, as well as others with sincerely-held religious convictions, is one thing; distinguishing between them is another. The task is made all the more difficult by the propaganda war which Muslim governments and Islamist groups wage against each other. Non-Muslim readers need to be aware that oppressive governments in the Muslim world are extremely skilled at using the media to rally western opinion in their favour by stigmatising Islamists as dangerous fanatics and enemies of democracy. Muslim readers, on the other hand, need to be aware that Islamists are equally skilled at manipulating Muslim youth through political oratory and pamphleteering which depict the leaders of Muslim states as unbelieving tyrants.

1962 to the Present: (d) Genuine Revival or Force of Circumstances?

Political and economic factors have loomed so large in the previous three sections that some readers may have begun to wonder whether there has been a genuine resurgence of Islam at all. If one were to take away the petro-dollars; Muslim disillusionment with nationalist leaders; western backing for Islamists during the Cold War; and anti-western feeling caused by conflicts in the Middle East, what would be left? I have dwelt on these factors at length because they have undoubtedly played an important role. Nevertheless, the reductionist thesis, that what appears to be a religious revival is in reality nothing but the product of material forces, is unprovable and seems quite improbable for two reasons. First, the revival has touched countless Muslims who stand aloof both from Islamism and from the various forms of state-sanctioned Islam. They include, for example, the members of the Sunni *Tablighi Jamaat*, the largest missionary movement in the Muslim World. This movement, which was founded in India by Muhammad Ilyas (1885–1944) now has branches in more than ninety countries. It is quietist and apolitical, and targets non-practising Muslims by encouraging them to observe six principles: the testimony of faith; prayer; the acquisition of knowledge of God and recollection of him; respect for every Muslim; sincerity of intention; and the devotion of part of one's time to preaching. Second, although national and international crises of various kinds have led many in the Muslim world to look to Islam for a solution to their problems, this in no way detracts from the value of the spiritual resources which they have discovered, or rediscovered, within it. It is these spiritual resources which we will now examine.

5 The Quran

Its Status

Muslims believe that the Quran is the uncreated Word of God which has existed in his presence from all eternity as 'the mother of the Book' (43.4), 'the preserved tablet' (85.22). It was brought down to the nearest heaven one Ramadan on the 'Night of Power' (97.1) and delivered orally to the Prophet Muhammad by the angel Gabriel (2.97) over a period of twenty-three years. The Prophet and his Companions committed the revelations to memory and recited them when they performed the prayers. The recitation had a profound effect on some of the hearers (17.107) but others dismissed Muhammad as merely a magician (10.2), poet (21.5) or soothsayer (69.42), and accused him of forgery (25.4f). Those who rejected the revelations as forgeries were repeatedly challenged to produce something similar (2.23, 10.28, 11.13). Their failure to do so led the believers to claim that the Quran is inimitable, and that its inimitability (*ijaz*) is proof of its divine origin.

This claim must seem odd to non-Muslims who, as often as not, find the Quran a rather dull book when they try to read it in translation. The Arabic Quran is, however, primarily an aural-oral phenomenon. It exhibits rhyme, rhythm, assonance, alliteration and other poetic qualities which are lost when it is rendered into English. One must hear it recited in the emotionally-charged atmosphere of the mosque to appreciate Pickthall's description of it as

that inimitable symphony, the very sounds of which move
men to tears and ecstasy.

(M. M. Pickthall, *The Meaning of the Glorious
Koran*, New York, Dorset Press n. d., p. vii)

Nevertheless, some Muslim scholars have questioned the
wisdom of attributing the inimitability of the Quran to its
sublime style. An-Nazzam (d. 846) argued that it is not
intrinsically inimitable, but God has prevented the Arabs from
imitating it by taking away their competence. Others have
suggested that its inimitability lies more in its contents, including
the detailed information which it gives about past events and the
last things.

Its Preservation

Non-Muslims often stress the absence of any tangible evidence
for the existence of the Quran before the inscriptions on the
Dome of the Rock, which were carved in 692. Some of them
argue that the revelations were transmitted orally over a long
period before they were eventually written down. My own
research on the literary structure of the Quran has, however,
convinced me that it is much more coherent than is generally
recognised, and that it is therefore unlikely that it is the product
of clumsily edited oral traditions. In this section, I shall simply
attempt to summarise the traditional Muslim accounts of how
the revelations were preserved, collected, and edited. As far as I
am concerned, whether or not these traditions are reliable
remains an open question.

According to tradition, as well as learning the revelations by
heart, some of the Companions jotted them down on loose leaves
as *aide mémoire*. Moreover, in the Medinan period the Prophet
deliberately employed scribes. Therefore, by the time Muhammad died, in 632, all the revelations had been memorised and
were also available in written form. What is more, the order of
the suras had been fixed, as had the order of ayas within each
sura. Nevertheless, the Quran as a whole had not yet been
collected into a book. The following year, however, a number of
Muslims who knew the Quran by heart were killed in the battle

of Yamama. The first Caliph, Abu Bakr, was consequently persuaded to have a manuscript prepared before any of the revelations were lost. The work was carried out by Zayd b. Thabit, who had been one of the Prophet's scribes. He produced a single written copy which remained in Abu Bakr's possession. When Abu Bakr died it passed to his successor Umar, and then to Umar's daughter Hafsa. By this time, serious disputes had arisen among the Muslims about the correct manner of reciting the Quran. The third Caliph, Uthman, therefore ordered Zayd and three other Companions to make perfect copies using Hafsa's manuscript as their basis. Identical copies were sent to the various provinces of the Muslim empire to replace other material which was in circulation, which Uthman ordered to be collected and burned. Uthman's promulgation of an authorised version of the Quran did not, however, put an end to the disagreement. There were two reasons for this. First, manuscripts attributed to several Companions including Ibn Masud and Ubayy survived in remote areas. These differed from Uthman's edition over the wording of some of the ayas. Second, in Uthman's edition the Arabic words were written without the vowels and could in some instances be vocalised in more than one way. Take for example the word *mlk* in 1.4. The majority of the scholars in Kufa read this with a long a as *mālik*, which gives the aya the meaning '*Master* of the Day of Recompense', whereas in Mecca, Medina, Damascus and Basra it was read as *malik* so that the aya was held to refer to God as '*Sovereign* of the Day of Recompense'. By 728, scholars in Basra had invented a method of indicating the vowels by inserting marks above and below the consonants, but by that time rival systems of reading were well established. A ninth-century scholar called Ibn Mujahid wrote a book entitled *The Seven Readings*. As a result of this work, the 'exceptional' readings attributed to Ibn Masud, Ubayy and other Companions, were finally outlawed because they differed from Uthman's consonantal text, and seven rival systems of vocalising that text, which were taught in the principal cities, were canonised on the grounds that the Prophet had said that the Quran was revealed in seven modes. The first printed edition of the Quran produced by Muslims was published in Egypt in 1925. In this edition, the text is vocalised in accordance with the system taught in Kufa by Hafs (d. 796). Most subsequent editions have been based on the standard Egyptian edition with the result that Hafs's system is now the only one in common use, except in North Africa, where another of the seven systems – that taught in Medina by Warsh (d. 812) – is still widely favoured.

The Chronology of the Revelations

The 114 suras of the Quran are not arranged in chronological order. It is generally held that the earliest revelation is the first part of Sura 96. It was brought to Muhammad one night in Ramadan, around the year 609, while he was meditating in a cave on a barren rocky hill outside Mecca

> Read in the name of thy Lord who created.
> He created Man from a blood clot.
> Read, and thy Lord is most generous,
> He who has taught with the pen,
> Taught Man what he knew not.

(96.1–5)

The final revelation is thought to be the third aya of Sura 5. It is said that it was revealed in 632, in the course of a sermon which the Prophet preached at Arafat while he was performing the pilgrimage for the last time

> This day the unbelievers despair of prevailing against your religion, so fear not them but fear Me. This day have I perfected your religion for you and it has been my good pleasure to choose Islam for you as your religion.

(5.3)

In the standard Egyptian edition each sura has a heading which states whether it was revealed during the Meccan or the Medinan period and names the sura that was revealed immediately before it. Some English translations, including those by Khatib and Irving, give these headings as if they were an integral part of the Quran. This is not the case. The headings are the work of the editors. Although they are based on ancient traditions, those traditions are far from unanimous. In short, there is not, nor ever has been, a consensus among Muslim scholars about the precise order in which the suras were revealed. Since the nineteenth century, several European scholars have attempted to determine the chronological order of the suras by using their own stylistic and theological criteria to supplement the Islamic traditions. Their efforts have met with only limited success. The scheme proposed by Theodor Nöldeke is a marginally better working hypothesis than the standard Egyptian chronology but it is clearly not the last word on the subject.

The Message of the Quran

Although, as I indicated in the previous paragraph, the precise order in which the suras were revealed is not known for certain, in most instances it is usually fairly clear from the contents of a given sura whether it was revealed during the Meccan or the Medinan period. In Mecca, the Prophet had only a small band of followers and was harassed by the rich and powerful Arab pagans. In Medina, on the contrary he was a religious and political leader for whom the Meccan pagans sometimes posed an external military threat, but for whom the day-to-day opposition came primarily from the Jewish elements of the population.

The central message of the Quran, which runs through both the Meccan and the Medinan suras, is that there is only one God and that he alone is to be worshipped and obeyed. Nevertheless, the Meccan and Medinan revelations differ in tenor and content.

The Meccan suras tend to be shorter than those revealed in Medina and to have relatively short ayas. They contain six principal types of material. First, there are what I call 'Messenger sections', because they are addressed primarily to Muhammad, the Messenger of God. In these ayas, or groups of ayas, God reveals Himself to Muhammad as his Lord, commissioning him (74.1–7); giving him instructions about his devotions (e.g. 73.1–9); comforting him (e.g. 93.3–8); and rebuking him (80.3–10). Second, there are 'signs sections'. These point to the wonders of God's creation as evidence of His beneficence, which should elicit gratitude (e.g. 55.1–25), and as evidence of His power, which ought to convince sceptics of His ability to raise the dead to life (e.g. 56.57–73; 75.36–40). Third, there are 'polemical sections' in which the Arab pagans are lambasted for worshipping other deities besides God (e.g. 53.19–23); for their love of material possessions (e.g. 103.1–3); for their failure to care for the more vulnerable members of society (e.g. 89.17–20); and for their rejection of the message, and their persecution of the believers (e.g. 96.9–13). Fourth, there are 'narrative sections'. Some of these relate how previous peoples who rejected God's messengers were consequently destroyed (e.g. 51.24–46). Others describe the exemplary lives of believers such as the patriarch Joseph (12.4–101), and Mary the mother of Jesus (19.16–33). Fifth, their are 'eschatological sections' which describe in graphic detail the impending cataclysm (e.g. 81.1–13); the last judgement (e.g. 99.4–8); the pleasures of Paradise and the torments of Hell (e.g. 69.19–34). Finally, there are what I call 'revelation sections' because they deal specifically with the revealed status of the message. They comprise statements about its authenticity (e.g. 53.4; 56.77–80), rebuttals of accusations levelled at the Prophet (e.g. 69.41, 44–46; 81.22); and accounts of his visions (53.5–10, 13–16, 18; 81.23).

The Medinan suras are often long and intricate. Nevertheless, we may begin by noting that they contain the six types of material found in the Meccan suras, albeit in a modified form. Messenger sections now frequently begin with the words 'O Prophet' (e.g. 8.64). Polemic against the Arab pagans is relatively rare and gives way to tirades against the unbelieving Jews (e.g. 4.153–161) and Christians (e.g. 5.72–75). The long eschatological passages aimed at convincing the sceptics are replaced by much simpler stereotyped allusions to Paradise and Hell which are addressed to the believers (e.g. 2.25, 81f). The narrative sections are no longer dominated by punishment stories about peoples who were utterly destroyed for their unbelief, but rather by stories of how God repeatedly forgave the Children of Israel in Moses' time after chastising them (e.g. 2.40–141 *passim*). Muhammad is now clearly portrayed as having the same status as Moses (2.108; 4.153) and of the other Hebrew prophets including Abraham and Jesus (e.g. 4.163). As the Medinan revelations are addressed primarily to Muslims, or to Jews and Christians who share their belief in Creation and the Hereafter, signs passages are no longer necessary although they are still found occasionally (e.g. 2.21–22, 28–29, 164). Finally, revelation sections are relatively rare (e.g. 2.1–2; 4.82; 24.1). In addition to these six types of material, the Medinan suras contain a profusion of legal precepts and exhortations intended specifically for the believing community (e.g. 2.178–203, 278–283; 4.1–12, 15–25, 29–43). Many of them also make frequent reference to God's names, in formulae such as 'He is the Oft-Relenting the Merciful' and 'He is All-Powerful All-Wise'.

It is obvious that in both Mecca and Medina the revelations were couched in terms which would appeal in the first instance to Muhammad's contempories: Hell is depicted as worse than a tropical desert in the heat of summer, with neither water nor shade, whereas Paradise sounds more enticing and refreshing than any earthly oasis; the narratives are about legendary Arab peoples or biblical characters with whom the Arabs were probably familiar through their contacts with Jews and Christians; and God's signs include date-palms and camels – the flora and fauna on which the Arabs depended most.

Despite this, the Meccan suras nevertheless convey a message which is of universal significance. Let us look again at each of the six types of material in turn, this time focussing on their present relevance. The Messenger sections inform us that the Prophet was not the author of the message but rather its faithful transmitter. The signs sections affirm that God is the sole Creator and that all around us there are abundant signs of His beneficence and power which should evoke our gratitude and awe. The polemical sections take human beings to task for their inclination to worship false gods who leave them free to indulge their selfishness and greed to the detriment of the weaker members of society. The narrative sections are a salutatory reminder that past civilisations which sank to that level of degradation, and which rejected the upright prophets and messengers who tried to call the people to their senses, have vanished almost without trace. The eschatological sections are a dire warning that our own society is heading the same way and that every individual will ultimately be held accountable for his or her own actions. Finally, the revelation sections reinforce the Messenger sections by indicating that the message originated with none other than the Creator.

Whereas the Meccan suras enunciate the basic principles of Islam, the Medinan suras furnish specific guidelines for establishing an Islamic society. Take for example the principle that we have been generously provided for by our Creator and are therefore under obligation to care for others rather than strive selfishly to amass more and more wealth. Knowledge of that principle is not in itself sufficient to save us from our greed. The Medinan revelations therefore command the payment of compulsory charity called *zakat*; they prohibit gambling and the charging of interest on loans, and they institute the fast of Ramadan as a means of inculcating self-restraint. Nevertheless, the non-Muslim may legitimately ask whether some of the Medinan legislation is either relevant or appropriate today. Prohibiting the consumption of pork makes eminent sense in tropical regions where parasites are rife but is it still necessary in temperate zones where parasites can more easily be controlled? Amputating the hands of thieves may have worked with the rude Arabian bedouin but do we not now have at our disposal more humane ways of reforming criminals? Allowing a man to have up to four wives was perhaps necessary in a warrior society where the women often far outnumbered the men, but is it appropriate in modern post-industrial societies where this is rarely the case? These are sensitive issues. For the moment let me simply make two points. On the one hand, most Muslims hold that in principle the specific commands and prohibitions found in the Quran express God's will for all time. On the other hand, it is generally recognised that the Quran is only one of the sources of the *Sharia*, the all-embracing Islamic legal system. The latter is, as its name suggests, a 'broad path', and in practice it is also often remarkably flexible, as we shall see in Chapter 12.

Quranic Interpretation

Because the Quran plays a central role in Islamic law, almost all famous quranic commentators have been first and foremost experts in Islamic jurisprudence. With their sharp legal minds and encyclopedic knowledge of tradition, they have scrutinised the sacred text seeking to fix the precise meaning of every word and phrase and to eliminate all traces of ambiguity. Still to this day, the most widely advocated approach to commenting on the Quran is *tafsir bi-l-mathur*, which may be translated loosely as 'exegesis on the basis of tradition'. This approach is epitomised by the commentary composed by the Syrian scholar Ibn Kathir (d. 1372). Building on the work of his teacher Ibn Taymiya, he argued that exegetes should follow a strict procedure drawing one by one on a hierarchy of authorities. To begin with, they should seek to interpret the Quran solely on the basis of the Quran. This requires a knowledge of the whole scripture together with a grasp of two fundamental principles established by earlier commentators. First, in view of the fact that the Quran itself (3.7) refers to the distinction between ayas whose meaning is clear (*muhkamat*) and others whose meaning is obscure to most people (*mutashabihat*), the latter should be interpreted by reference to the former. Second, apparent contradictions in the legal material are to be explained in terms of abrogation (*naskh*, see 2.106). For instance, we must assume that the command not to pray while drunk (4.43) has been abrogated by the subsequent total prohibition of wine (5.90f). After attempting to interpret the Quran in the light of the Quran, exegetes should next turn to the Sunna as preserved in the hadiths – reports of what the Prophet said, did, and tacitly approved or disapproved – to see what bearing this has on the passage they are studying. Then, after the Sunna, there are the comments of the Companions – the Muslims who knew the Prophet during his life-time and who may therefore be assumed to have known his mind. Failing that, the sayings of their pupils, the Successors, may be taken into account provided they are not contradictory. Finally, exegetes may draw on their knowledge of Arabic grammar and lexicography. Ibn Kathir was a Sunni Muslim, but a similar approach is advocated by many of the Shia, except that they have their own collections of hadiths and for them the statements of the Imams are more authoritative than those of the Companions and Successors.

As a way of interpreting the Quranic commands and prohibitions, exegesis on the basis of tradition may seem reasonable enough. Unfortunately, however, its application to the Quran as a whole has tended to mask the fact that the Quran is a highly poetic book which seeks to transform the human consciousness by opening up the reader's horizons rather than to confine him to a mental strait-jacket. Moreover, in Chapter 7 we shall see that there are grounds for doubting the authenticity of many of the traditions allegedly traced back to the Prophet and his Companions. It should also be borne in mind that there are other approaches to quranic commentary which have a respectable pedigree. These approaches are usually grouped together under the umbrella term *tafsir bi-r-ray*, 'exegesis on the basis of informed opinion', although they are quite varied. For instance, the ninth-century Iraqi grammarians wrote brief commentaries based almost exclusively on their knowledge of the Arabic language, whereas the polymath Fakhr ad-Din ar-Razi (d. 1210) drew on his encyclopedic knowledge of a wide range of disciplines and evaluated the comments of his predecessors on the basis of their plausibility rather than their antiquity. Even the celebrated Sunni theologian al-Ghazali (d. 1111) recognised the scope for *tafsir bi-r-ray*, for he played down the importance of the comments attributed to the Companions on the grounds that they were after all only their opinions.

The Coherence of the Quran

Because of their legal training, most of the classical commentators treated the Quran as if it were a collection of propositions. Their primary concern was with the meaning of words and sentences rather than the relationship between consecutive ayas or consecutive suras. European students of Islam, on the other hand, have often tried to read the Quran from cover to cover as if it were a work of literature and have generally found it wanting. The essayist Thomas Carlyle, for example, dismissed it as 'toilsome reading' and 'a wearisome confused jumble'. He may perhaps be excused on the grounds that he had at his disposal only a rather dull English translation, but what are we to make of the fact that several distinguished Arabists have also judged the Quran to lack structure and coherence? The alleged deficiencies are threefold. Let us examine them one at a time.

First, there is apparent incoherence at the level of individual ayas or small groups of ayas. Nöldeke drew attention in particular to the frequency with which the speaker chops and changes, referring to himself as 'I', 'We' and 'He', as in the following passage

No! I swear by the Lord of the Eastern places and the
Western places that We are able to replace them with
someone better than they are. We shall never be overruled.

(70.40f)

He concluded that Muhammad was simply a bad stylist who
tried to give the impression that he was being addressed by God
but could not maintain this fiction and frequently lapsed into
making statements about Him. What he failed to notice was that
the abrupt changes in pronoun are a rhetorical device which
enhances the effect of the utterances and that the speaker's use of
different pronouns as self-designations is perfectly consistent. He
employs the first person singular 'I', 'Me', 'My' when He wishes
to be particularly intimate with His servants; when He wishes to
express His wrath; or when He wishes to safeguard His divine
unity. He employs the first person plural 'We', 'Us', 'Our' when
He wishes to express His power, majesty or generosity. Finally
He uses the third person singular 'He', 'Him', 'His', or refers to
Himself as 'God', 'Lord' and so on, when He wishes to convey
information about Himself which is to be repeated by the
believers. For instance, if the words 'by the Lord of the Eastern
places and the Western places' were omitted from the ayas
quoted above, the ayas would still make sense but their
universality would be diminished.

Second, many suras seem to lack an overall structure. Richard
Bell was especially concerned by the sudden changes of subject
matter: from eschatology to narrative to instructions addressed
to the Prophet and so forth. He argued that, because of the
shortage of writing materials, revelations were often written on
the reverse side of sheets which had already been used to record
earlier revelations or discarded first drafts. The editors failed to
realise this and copied out the two sides consecutively, thereby
producing suras which were composed of unrelated fragments. I
have elsewhere examined some of the suras which Bell found
disjointed and have demonstrated that on closer examination
they prove to be much more unified that he realised. They are in
fact held together by rhyme and rhythm and by the recurrence of
key words. The rhyme and rhythm are of course largely lost
when the Quran is rendered into English but the recurrence of
key words may still be detected by the astute reader provided

the translation he uses is reasonably consistent. One simple example must suffice. 2.282 is a very long aya – a whole page in most editions – which instructs the believers that when they contract a debt for a set period they should have it recorded in writing. Although it deals with a matter of law and occurs near the end of the sura, it echoes material dealing with revelation which occurs near the beginning. For instance it contains repeated reference to writing and scribes (words derived from the Arabic verb *kataba*) and asserts that the practice of writing a contract and having it witnessed reduces doubt. This is reminiscent of what is said in the prologue of the sura about the Quran: it is a Book or Scripture (Arabic *kitab*) in which there is no doubt (2.2) and those who are in doubt about what has been revealed are challenged to produce a sura like it and call on their witnesses (2.23).

Third, apart from the fact that the suras are arranged approximately in accordance with decreasing length, there seems to be no obvious rationale for their present order. Two English translators, one Christian and the other Jewish, have therefore taken it upon themselves to improve on the traditional order. Rodwell opted to arrange the suras chronologically. Dawood's translation, on the other hand

> begins with the more Biblical and poetic passages and ends with the much longer, and often more topical, chapters.
>
> (N. J. Dawood, *The Koran*, Harmondsworth,
> Penguin, 4th ed. 1974, p. 11)

In a statement which earned him a citation in Andrew Veitch's *Naked Ape: an anthology of male chauvism from the Guardian*, Dawood alleged that the new arrangement was

> primarily intended for the uninitiated reader who, under-standably, is often put off by such mundane chapters as 'The Cow' or 'Women' which are traditionally placed at the beginning of the book.
>
> (ibid)

However, the suras are not chapters and their names are not chapter headings. Dawood's introduction is therefore very misleading. The word sura is used only in the Quran and refers exclusively to the 114 suras contained in it. The sura names are simply convenient ways of identifying them. For example Sura 2, 'The Cow' is not primarily about a cow but it is given this name because the noun 'cow' occurs four times in 2.67–71 and is not found in the singular in any other sura. The relationship between consecutive suras is still not perfectly understood but it is certainly not random as Rodwell, Dawood and many other scholars suppose. This should be obvious from the fact that key words or notions which occur near the end of one sura are frequently taken up near the beginning of the next. Consider for example the first three suras. Sura 1 ends with the petition 'guide is in the straight path. . .' (1.7) and Sura 2 begins with a reference to the Quran as a 'guidance for the godfearing'; Sura 2 reaches a crescendo in the celebrated throne verse which opens 'God, there is no god but He, the Living the Everlasting' (2.255), and this sentence is repeated word for word at the beginning of Sura 3 (3.2).

The Quran in English

Ideally, a good translation ought to be accurate, consistent, of literary merit and easy to consult. There are over 40 English translations of the Quran but none of them is entirely satisfactory because none of them meets all four criteria. Let us consider the last criterion first. The reader who comes across references to Quranic passages in a book and then tries to look them up in a translation may experience a certain amount of frustration. It is usually easy enough to locate the suras but the ayas are likely to cause difficulties. This is because several different systems of numbering the ayas are in use. Yusuf Ali and Pickthall used two different Indian systems and their numbering consequently differs occasionally from that of the standard Egyptian edition by one or two ayas. The recent revisions of Yusuf Ali's translation sponsored independently by King Fahd and the Amana Corporation have, however, rectified this. More seriously, Bell and Arberry based their translations on an Arabic edition of the Quran published in Leipzig by the Orientalist Gustav Flügel, and consequently their numbering is sometimes out of step by up to seven ayas. In addition, Bell cuts the suras into sections and sometimes prints two consecutive sections in parallel columns to illustrate his views about the disorderly way in which the revelations were edited. The older translation by Sale is regrettably even less user-friendly because he did not number the ayas at all.

As regards literary style, the translation by Ahmed Ali, the Pakistani novelist and poet, is sublime. Unfortunately, however, it is wildly inaccurate and very inconsistent. The only other translations which attempt to capture some of the poetic qualities of the original are those by Arberry and Yusuf Ali. Arberry's translation may be recommended for its rhythmic qualities although readers may find the Edwardian English somewhat quaint. Like Arberry, Yusuf Ali occasionally employs assonance and alliteration. In addition, he splits the longer ayas into short lines and arranges them in blocks rather like stanzas of poetry. Sometimes his subdivisions correspond to the Arabic clauses but this is not always the case. For those who prefer straightforward modern prose, Fakhry, Dawood and Irving are serviceable although English readers may find that the Irvings's American idiom jars with them at times. One of the drawbacks of using these modern translations is that they sometimes blur the distinction between passages which are addressed to the Prophet and passages which are addressed to groups of people: believers, unbelievers, Jews and Christians. The distinction is clearer in Pickthall and Abdul Majid Daryabadi because, like Yusuf Ali and Arberry, they employ the old-fashioned second person singular pronouns thou, thee and thy.

Because the repetition of key words and phrases is one of the unifying factors in individual suras and in the Quran as a whole, consistency is highly desirable. Unfortunately, however, the only translation which meets this criterion is Arberry's. In some of the others – including those by Yusuf Ali and Pickthall which are very popular – key terms are often translated in three or four different ways. Moreover, even when two whole ayas are identical in the Arabic, these translators sometimes render them differently.

When judged on the basis of accuracy, Arberry's translation is again by far and away the best. Those by Yusuf Ali, Abdul Majid Daryabadi, Irving, Dawood, Palmer, Pickthall, and Khatib are reasonably reliable, although Palmer and Pickthall make occasional errors because of their inadequate grasp of Arabic grammar, and Khatib's English is defective at times. Most of the other translations need to be treated with caution because of the presence of a marked sectarian or ideological bias. Shakir, Fakhry and S. V. Mir Ahmed Ali understood the Quran from a Shiite perspective although this only affected their rendering of a handful of ayas. Much more seriously, Zafrulla Khan was an Ahmadiyya and his work is a highly tendencious paraphrase from beginning to end. Sale and Rodwell occasionally sank to anti-Muslim polemic, although this is mostly confined to their introductions and notes. Khalili and Muhsin Khan were ultra-traditionalists. Their translation contains numerous glosses which are printed in brackets and which give an accurate picture of how the Quran was interpreted in the Middle Ages by scholars like Ibn Kathir, but which are misleading if they are taken as determining its meaning for all time. For example 24.31, an aya which deals with female modesty, is glossed to mean that a woman should leave no part of her body exposed except the palms of her hands and one eye – or both if she needs to see where she is going! Most of the other translators are modernists of one sort or another. Sometimes this manifests itself in their attempt to make the legal material more palatable to readers who have had a European education, an approach pioneered by Sayyid Ahmad Khan in nineteenth-century India. Asad does this occasionally but usually with some justification. For instance, whereas 5.33f has traditionally been understood as stipulating the Islamic penalty for sedition, he interprets it quite plausibly as a description of what non-Muslims were doing to each other. Ahmed Ali, on the other hand, goes to extremes; he frequently distorts the meaning of the text, for example by replacing wife-beating with love-making (4.34), as well as eliminating amputation as the punishment for theft (5.38) and introducing an allusion to family planning (2.223)! Modernism may also take the form of scientific rationalism. This too, may be traced to the influence of Sayyid Ahmad Khan. Its exponents seek to minimise the miraculous and folkloric elements. Asad does this occasionally but the prime culprits are Zafrulla Khan and Ahmed Ali. In their translations, Jesus does not create living birds from clay (3.49); rather, he shapes people's destiny and breathes new life into them so that they rise like birds. Nor does Solomon have supernatural powers which enable him to understand the speech of birds and ants (27.16–44); he is simply a good linguist who has mastered the languages of tribes called Tayr (Birds) and Naml (Ants). Finally, some modernists are champions of so-called 'scientific exegesis' and claim to find references to modern scientific discoveries. They do this out of a desire to prove the Quran's supernatural origins by showing that it refers to things which could not possibly have been known by human beings in the time of Muhammad. The translation by Dr and Mrs Zidan is the most thoroughgoing in this respect. They imply for instance that the Quran gives a physiological explanation of how milk is produced (16.66) and mentions that the universe is still expanding (51.47). Traces of scientific exegesis are also present in the translations by Asad, Ahmed Ali and Khatib.

For the reasons given above, it is not easy to recommend an English translation of the Quran. Arberry's *The Koran Interpreted* scores highest on three criteria out of four but is difficult to consult. It has to be read in conjunction with another version in which the ayas are correctly numbered. Alternatively, the reader may locate passages by using the conversion table in my book, *Discovering the Qur'an*, pp. 288–90. After Arberry, the revised version of Yusuf Ali's *The Meaning of the Holy Qur'an*, published by the Amana Corporation, is probably the next best translation, although it falls down badly on the criterion of consistency. The so-called translations by Zafrulla Khan and Ahmed Ali should be avoided at all cost.

No God but God

Introduction

I shall begin this chapter by describing the connotations which *Allah*, the Arabic word for God, had in pre-Islamic Arabia. Then I shall attempt to give a summary of the quranic teaching about God. This will be followed by brief discussions of God in Islamic theology, Islamic philosophy, Sufism and the thought of Mawdudi. My treatment of these four topics will inevitably be selective but it should suffice to indicate the range of ways in which Muslims have interpreted their testimony that 'there is no god but God'.

Allah in Pre-Islamic Arabia

The word *Allah* is an abbreviation of *al-ilah*, which simply means 'the god'. The Quran implies that the Arab pagans recognised the existence of Allah but thought of him as a remote deity or high god who was of little relevance to their everyday lives. When pressed, they acknowledged that he was the Creator (23.84–9, 29.61–3, 39.38); and in times of crisis, such as life-threatening storms at sea, they would even pray to him directly (10.22, 29.65). He was not, however, in their view, the sole deity, for they ascribed daughters to him, including the goddesses al-Lat, Manat, al-Uzza (37.149f, 53.19–21). In most circumstances it was to them and other associates of His that they appealed for help (6.136, 10.18 etc.). Moreover, they did not believe that Allah determined the duration of their lives; that he made moral demands on them; or that he would reward or punish them in the hereafter. At heart, they were fatalists whose attitude is summed up in their claim that 'there is only our present life. We die and we live, and only time destroys us.' (45.24).

Not all the inhabitants of pre-Islamic Arabia were pagans; there were Arabic-speaking Jews and Christians as well. They too called God *Allah*, but we may infer from the Quran that some of them had unorthodox beliefs about Him. The Jews of Arabia apparently regarded Uzayr (Ezra?) as Allah's son (9.30), and some of the Christians identified Jesus with Allah (5.72), whereas others seem to have worshipped a divine triad in which Allah was thought of as the Father, Mary the Mother, and Jesus the Son (5.116). In addition, a number of Muslim writers mention the existence of a few unaligned monotheists known as *hanifs*. They held that Allah was the sole deity but they were neither Jews nor Christians.

The Witness of the Quran

The Quran mentions Allah 2,692 times and asserts repeatedly that there is no god besides Him (27.26, 47.19, 52.22 etc.). Against the mistaken beliefs of Arab pagans, Christian tritheists and Zoroastrian dualists, it declares that He is One (2.163, 4.171, 5.73, 16.51, 112.1 etc.) and has neither associates (10.66, 13.16 etc.) nor offspring (2.116, 10.68, 112.3 etc.). The various names which the Quran ascribes to Allah stress not only His unity, but also His eternity ('First', 'Last', 'Heir', 'Living'); His perfection ('Self-sufficient', 'Worthy of all praise'); His omnipotence ('All-mighty', 'All-powerful'); His omniscience ('All-knowing', 'All-wise', 'All-seeing', 'All-hearing', 'Totally-aware'); His reliability ('Patron', 'Trustee'); His beneficence ('All-merciful', 'All-pitying', 'Bene-volent'); and His indulgence ('All-forgiving', 'Oft-relenting').

Allah's activity is all-encompassing. He alone is the Creator (13.16 etc.) and He made the heavens and the earth out of nothing (2.117, 6.101). He remains in total control of His creation: by His power He keeps the birds in flight (16.79), and it is He who sends the rains and causes the crops to grow in order to provide mankind with food (e.g. 2.22). Moreover, He never tires of his task (2.255). He participates in human history: it was He, for instance, who foiled the attempt of an invading army to destroy the Kaaba (109.1–5), and he who helped the Muslims in the Battle of Badr (8.11–17). He is concerned to provide human beings with moral guidance (92.12 etc). The blind fatalism of the pre-Islamic Arabs is countered by the Quran's assertion that Allah determines when we are born, what calamities will befall us, and when we shall die (45.26, 57.22). He knows everything we do (6.59f) and not even our innermost thoughts escape Him (50.17). He will raise the dead to life (e.g. 19.66–8) and judge them according to their deeds (e.g. 7.8f, 101.6–9).

Islamic Theology

When Islam spread beyond Arabia into the great cultural centres which had once been part of the Byzantine and Persian empires, Muslims encountered philosophers and Christian theologians who forced them to think about their faith in a more analytical way. The origins of Islamic scholastic theology (*kalam*) are still disputed, but the first major school about which we have substantial information is that of the **Mutazilites**, whose thought probably began to take shape in the last quarter of the eighth century. They were concerned to give a rational account of Islam and to safeguard the unity and justice of God. A key problem which exercised their minds was the relationship between God's essence and His attributes. The Quran speaks of God as Living, All-knowing, All-powerful and so on. Does this imply that He possesses the attributes of life, knowledge and power? Surely not, they argued, for if that were the case there would be an element of plurality in the Godhead. They therefore maintained that there was no distinction between God's essence and His attributes, and one Mutazilite even went as far as declaring that 'God knows by his knowledge, and knowledge is his essence'. Another problem which the Mutazilites grappled with was the widespread assumption that the Quran was eternal. They argued that this could not possibly be correct because it would imply the existence of two eternal entities: God and his Word. Instead, they maintained that although the Quran had existed in the guarded tablet before it was revealed to Muhammad (85.21f), it had nonetheless been created by God. The Mutazilites also reacted very strongly against the popular belief that God had a body, for this too seemed to undermine the divine unity because bodies are never entirely homogeneous. Hence they insisted that the quranic references to God's hands, face and throne must be interpreted as metaphors for his power, his essence and his knowledge, and that on the Day of Resurrection the believers would see God in their hearts rather than with their physical eyes. As far as divine justice was concerned, the main issue was free will. The quranic stress on God's absolute omnipotence led many to infer that human affairs were entirely predetermined by him. Against this, the Mutazilites insisted that human beings must have a measure of free will for otherwise God would be unjust in punishing evildoers and rewarding the righteous.

Some of the key beliefs of the Mutazilites were adopted by the all the main branches of the Shiites, especially the Zaydis. In recent times, a number of Sunni intellectuals have also championed them. In mainstream Sunni circles, however, they went out of favour during the tenth century when they were gradually superseded by the doctrines of the **Asharites**. Asharism, which is the predominant school of theology in contemporary Sunnism, began as a broad movement of reaction against the excessive rationalism of the Mutazilites but it was given shape by al-Ashari (d. 935), who dramatically renounced his Mutazilite background. Al-Ashari maintained that the divine attributes are distinct from the essence. He argued that if this were not so, we would be justified in invoking Knowledge rather than invoking God. Nevertheless, he insisted that terms used of human beings must have quite different meanings when applied to God: God's knowledge is qualitatively different from human knowledge, it does not simply differ in degree. The same is true of his hands, face and so on. We simply have to accept this without asking how. He denied that the Quran had been created, on the grounds that the Quran itself distinguishes between God's creation and his command (7.54), and that if God had created his Word by addressing a word to it (2.117) one would have to suppose that that word had itself been created by a word, and so on *ad infinitum*. He defended belief in the beatific vision on the grounds that it was implied in the Quran (75.22f) and in a hadith in which the Prophet said 'You will see your

Lord as you see the full moon.' Al-Ashari's most subtle and creative thinking was on the issue of free will and predestination. He argued that God creates in his creatures both the power to perform an act and the choice to perform it. Then He creates the action corresponding to the power and choice. Though the action is created by God, it is 'acquired' or 'earned' by the creature (cp. 2.286), who is therefore held responsible for it. What this boils down to is that we are free in so far as we feel free and that we are held responsible for our actions because we feel responsible for them.

Islamic Philosophy

The influence of Greek thought on the scholastic theologians was only slight, being evident, for instance, in their acceptance of the terms 'essence' and 'attribute' and in their use of Aristotelian logic. Greek philosophy was, however, taught in Abbasid Iraq both in Gunde-Shapur (150 km north-east of Basra), where hellenistic education had previously thrived under the Persians, and in Baghdad, where Caliph al-Mamun (813–33) established an institution called *Bayt al-Hikma* ('the House of Wisdom'), which was a major centre for the translation and preservation of Greek texts. In these circumstances, it is hardly surprising that in the ninth century there emerged a class of Muslim intellectuals who regarded themselves as full-blown philosophers. They were mostly physicians or administrators who had studied Greek philosophy as an adjunct to medicine or political science. Their religious beliefs never gained wide acceptance, but I mention them here in order to emphasise the tolerant nature of medieval Islam. Ibn Sina (d. 1037), who is better known in Europe as Avicenna, was fairly typical. He denied that God created the world out of nothing, and argued instead that he was responsible for its form but not its substance. As a good Aristotelian, he also denied that God could have knowledge of particulars, because such knowledge is based on sensory input and sensory input requires a body. Finally, he believed in the immortality of the soul and regarded the quranic references to the resurrection of the body as pictorial language intended for the common people.

The last great Islamic philosopher in the Sunni world was Ibn Rushd (d. 1198). After his death, philosophy became marginalised in the Arab lands east of Iraq. In the Shiite world, however, where it is closely associated with theology, it has continued to play a significant role down to the present day.

Sufism

Although there are traditions tracing Sufism back to the time of the Prophet, non-Muslim scholars generally assume that it began as a reaction against the worldliness of Umayyad society, at a time when most people seemed to have lost sight of the ideals of early Islam. **The first Sufis** were world-denying ascetics who lived in constant fear of hell and wore coarse garments made of wool (Arabic *suf*). Very soon, however, possibly to some extent in opposition to Mutazilism, which reduced God to an intellectual abstraction, the Sufis came to stress God's immanence and His love for His creatures. In so doing, they were building on aspects of the quranic teaching which had previously been relatively neglected. For in the Quran, God declares that He is nearer to man than his jugular vein (50.16); He refers to Himself as the Most-loving (*wadud*, 11.90, 85.14); and He mentions a people whom He will love and who will love Him (5.54). The person who introduced this new emphasis into Sufism was probably Rabia of Basra (d. 801), the celebrated woman mystic to whom we owe the following beautiful prayer

> O God, if I worship thee in fear of hell, burn me in hell; if I worship thee in hope of paradise, exclude me from paradise; but if I worship thee for thine own sake, withold not thy everlasting beauty.

In a similar vein, she is reputed to have walked through the streets of her home town carrying a lighted torch and a pitcher of water, declaring that she desired to set fire to paradise and quench the flames of hell.

In the course of the ninth century, the Sufis' stress on God's immanence and divine love gave rise to **the doctrines of *fana* and *baqa*,** 'passing away' and 'abiding' (cp. 55.26f). Sufis now sought to reach such perfection in this life that they 'passed away' by losing consciousness of the self and becoming absorbed into God, in whom they hoped to 'abide' or subsist after death. A number of ninth- and tenth-century Sufis are credited with extatic utterances which are interpreted as implying a momentary experience of *fana*. Two of the most famous are, 'Glory be to me! How great is my majesty!' and 'I am the Truth!' The former is attributed to Abu Yazid al-Bistami (d. 875) and the latter to Ibn Mansur al-Hallaj (d. 922). Practitioners of this 'intoxicated' Sufism frequently came under suspicion of heresy and several of them, including al-Hallaj, were executed by the authorities. More sober-minded Sufis of the following generations sought to rehabilitate the movement by writing manuals mapping out the Sufi journey through life in a series of 'stations', or stages of spiritual attainment on the way to God. The most famous Sufi treatise of this sort is the *Risala* of al-Qushairi (d. 1074) but the credit for finally reconciling Sufism with orthodox Sunni Islam is usually given to Abu Hamid al-Ghazali (d. 1111).

The principal Sufi Orders, or *tariqas* (literally 'ways'), came into existence during the twelfth and thirteenth century. They are widespread networks of disciples (*murids*), who have sworn allegiance to the same elder (*shaikh*), whom they revere as the spiritual heir of the founder. Each *tariqa* has its own discipline and ritual. The latter includes a *dhikr* (literally 'remembrance'). This is a set formula, including one or more of God's names, which they repeat over and over again. The most ancient *tariqas* are the Qadiriya, named after Abd al-Qadir Jilani (d. 1166); the Suhrawardiya, named after Shihab ad-Din Umar b. Abdallah as-Suhrawardi (d. 1234); the Shadhiliya, named after Abu al-Hasan Ali ash-Shadhili (d. 1258); and the Mevleviya, popularly known as the 'whirling dervishes', who refer to the Persian poet Jalaluddin Rumi as Mawlana ('Our Master') and look to him as their founder. Members of an order often spend a period studying in a monastery (*khanqa*) with their sheikh but they are not as a rule celibate, monkery being frowned on in Islam.

The Spanish mystic **Muhyi ad-Din Ibn al-Arabi** (d. 1240) did not found a *tariqa*. Despite this, his influence on Sufism has been enormous. He is often dismissed by his opponents as a pantheist – someone who believes that God is everything and everything is God. This is, however, a gross oversimplification. He taught what subsequent writers referred to as *wahdat al-wujud*, which may be rendered into English as 'the unity of existence' or 'existential monism'. In his view, although the divine Essence is absolutely unknowable, the universe as a whole manifests God's attributes. Moreover, since these attributes require the creation for their expression, the One is driven continually to transform itself into Many. Ibn al-Arabi's teaching has been condemned by many Sunni jurists, not least the fourteenth-century reformer Ibn Taymiya, who said that he was inspired by a Satanic spirit. Nevertheless, it undoubtedly facilitated the spread of Islam in India and south-east Asia amongst Hindus who believed that God was present in everything. Moreover, although Ibn al-Arabi was a Sunni, he has had many Shiite admirers, including the late Ayatollah Khomeini who recommended President Gorbachev to study his works!

Popular Sufism owes little to the teaching of the great Sufi masters and even less to the Quran. It thrives amongst Muslims from rural areas, where Islam has absorbed elements from Hinduism or animism. Many Muslims believe that they obtain *baraka* (Arabic 'blessing') by visiting the tombs of saints. A common practice is to tie rags or pieces of wool to the grill screening a tomb, or to a nearby tree, and to vow to make a donation or offer a sacrifice if one's prayers are answered as a result of the saint's intercession. In the world-famous *dargah* (Persian 'court') of Muin ad-Din Chisti at Ajmer in India, visitors are encouraged to kiss the threshold of the tomb. In theory, their motive is respect rather than worship, and they do not actually prostrate themselves, because their foreheads and noses do not touch the ground when they go down on their hands and knees. In practice, however, the theological distinction between a *sajda* (Arabic 'prostration') and a *bosa* (Persian 'kiss') is probably far from clear to many of the simple folk who perform this ritual in the belief that the saint is a living presence within his tomb.

Mawdudi's Understanding of the First Half of the Shahada

According to the Indo-Pakistani Islamist Abu 'l-Ala Mawdudi (d. 1970), *ilah* does not simply mean 'god'. Rather, it denotes anyone who has authority over others. Hence it is misleading to render *la ilaha illa llah* as 'there is no god but God'. In his view, the idolator is not the only person who recognises another *ilah* besides *Allah*; anyone who regards the word of someone else as worthy of obedience, without any sanction from Allah, is equally guilty. Thus Mawdudi denied that a person who is truly a Muslim can blindly follow the teaching of Sufi sheikhs or traditionalist ulama, or owe allegiance to any secular government or ideology.

7 Muhammad the Messenger of God

Introduction

There are references to Muhammad in early non-Muslim writings including an Armenian chronicle written in the 660s by Bishop Sebeos. His existence as a historical figure is therefore established beyond all reasonable doubt. Nevertheless, most of our information about him is drawn from works preserved or composed by Muslims: the Quran, the Hadith and the traditional biographies. In this chapter, I shall examine each of these in turn, so as to indicate their limitations as historical sources. Then I shall discuss the evidence for what non-Muslims have traditionally considered to be Muhammad's moral failings. This will be followed by a brief survey of his place in Muslim devotion. Finally, the chapter will end with a discussion of the relationship between prophets, messengers, Imams and saints. No attempt will be made to summarise Muhammad's career as this has already been done in Chapter 3.

Muhammad in the Quran

The Quran is our most ancient source. Unfortunately for our purposes, however, it mentions Muhammad by name only four times (3.144, 33.40, 47.2, 48.29) and yields very little hard biographical information about him. We learn from it that he was an orphan (93.6) who had originally been poor (93.8); that he began to receive revelations relatively late in life (10.16) and twice saw the revelatory angel (53.5–18); that he was expelled

from his home town (47.13); that he emigrated and married several women (33.50); but that he remained without male heir (33.40 cf. 108.3). The city to which he emigrated was Yathrib (33.6,13,40), also known as Medina (33.60). In view of the fact that the unbelieving kinsfolk of those who emigrated with him did not accompany them, but remained in the vicinity of 'the inviolable place of worship' (9.19–23), which seems to have been in or near Mecca (48.24f), we may reasonably surmise that Mecca was his home town.

Despite the paucity of biographical information, a great deal is said or implied about Muhammad's status. He is addressed as Prophet (8.64 etc.) and Messenger (5.41), and mentioned in the same breath as Noah, Abraham, Moses and Jesus (42.13). He is also described as 'the seal of the prophets' (33.40) and 'the unlettered prophet' (7.157). Non-Muslim scholars sometimes take these expressions to mean 'the one who confirmed the message of the previous prophets', and 'the prophet who arose among the gentiles, the people without scripture'. Muslims, however, generally assume that they mean that he was the final prophet, and that he was unable to read and write. Whether or not he was illiterate, we are clearly meant to infer from the following passage that he was not the author of the Quran but the passive recipient of the revelations

Do not move thy tongue with it to hasten it.
Ours it is to gather it and recite it.
So when We recite it, follow its recitation.

(75.16ff cp. 69.44–47)

In addition to being sent to teach the Scripture which was revealed to him, he was also sent to impart 'wisdom' (2.146). The believers are therefore exhorted to obey him and to follow his example

O you who believe, obey God and His Messenger.

(8.20)

When God and His Messenger have decreed a certain matter, it is not for a believing man or woman to have a choice in a matter affecting him.

(33.36)

> Whatever the Messenger gives you, take it, and whatever he forbids you abstain from it.
>
> (59.7)

> Verily, in the Messenger God you have a good example.
>
> (33.21)

Moreover, the Quran informs the believers that God and his angels send blessings upon Muhammad, and it urges them to do likewise (33.56). That is why Muslims often say 'peace and blessings be upon him' (sometimes written PBUH) when they mention his name.

Although the Quran ascribes a high status to Muhammad, it indicates that he was nonetheless a human being like those to whom he was sent: he had to eat food (25.7); was unable to perform the miracles which were requested of him (7.109, 13.7, 13.38); needed to ask God's forgiveness (40.55, 47.19, 48.2); and might one day die or be killed (3.144).

The Hadith

As the Quran refers to Muhammad as a teacher of wisdom and a role model for the believers, it is hardly surprising that some of the Companions and Successors made their own collections of his sayings. The sayings are referred to individually as hadiths, and collectively as the Hadith. Most of the early collections have perished because they were superseded by the much more comprehensive collections which were made in the ninth century. These are of two principal types: the *musnad*, in which the hadiths are classified on the basis of the Companions who transmitted them, and the *musannaf*, in which they are arranged in accordance with their subject matter. The former type is exemplified by the *Musnad* of Ibn Hanbal (d. 845), which contains 30,000 hadiths narrated by some 800 Companions. The most famous *musannafs* are the *Sahih* of Bukhari (d. 870) and the *Sahih* of Muslim b. al-Hajjaj (d. 874). Bukhari recorded 9,082 hadiths, including 6,480 repetitions, whereas Muslim recorded 7,275, including 3,275 repetitions. Each hadith has two components: an *isnad*, or chain of guarantors reaching back to a

Companion, and a *matn* or main text. The following example from Bukhari is typical

Al-Humaydiyy told us Sufyan told us saying I heard az-Zuhri say Ubaydallah Ibn Abdallah informed me on the authority of Ibn Abbas that he heard Umar say from the pulpit, I heard the Prophet of God say: 'Do not extol me as the Christians have extolled the Son of Mary. I am only God's servant. Refer to me as the Servant and Messenger of God'.

The *matn* need not necessarily be a saying. It can also be a brief anecdote about the Prophet or a statement about what he tacitly approved or disapproved, for example,

The Messenger of God never sat at a table.

Occasionally, the *matn* is an extra-Quranic revelation related by Muhammad, as in the following instance

Each night, when the night is two thirds spent, our blessed and exalted Lord descends to the lower heaven and says, 'If anyone invokes me, I will answer his prayer. If anyone asks me for something, I will grant it him. If anyone seeks forgiveness, I will forgive him.'

A hadith of this kind is called a *hadith qudsi*. Although it is regarded as divine revelation, it is never recited in prayer like the Quran.

By the time Bukhari and Muslim compiled their collections, many spurious hadiths had come into circulation. Some were invented for political reasons, for instance in support of the Umayyads or Abbasids; some out of malice, by people who wished to discredit Islam; some for religious motives – by Shiites, by believers in free will, or by ascetics who wished to encourage works of piety. Finally, there is evidence of people fabricating hadiths for financial gain – story-tellers who made a living by spinning good yarns, and merchants who boosted trade by alleging that the Prophet loved pumpkins or whatever else they were trying to sell. The Hadith collectors were well aware of this problem so they and subsequent scholars developed the science of hadith criticism to help them separate the wheat from the chaff. This involved scrutinising the *isnads*. It was necessary to identify every person in a given chain and establish that he or she was orthodox, honest, and of sound memory. It was also necessary to ascertain when and where they all lived so as to verify that the first person could have been a pupil of the second, the second of the third, and so on. Hadiths with impeccable *isnads* were classified as 'sound' (*sahih*). The others were deemed 'fair' (*hasan*), 'weak' (*daif*) or 'inauthentic' (*munkar*), depending on the extent of the deficiencies. The criteria varied slightly from writer to writer but the general principles were agreed: in the absence of a 'sound' hadith, one which was 'fair' would suffice to establish a point of law; 'weak' hadiths had no legal value but could be used for exhortation; and 'inauthentic' hadiths were to be rejected.

The fabric of traditional Islamic societies owes even more to the Hadith than it does to the Quran. The way in which Muslims in these societies pray, conduct business, wage war, marry and divorce, rear their children, dress, greet one another, eat and drink, or attend to matters of personal hygiene, are all largely determined by what the Prophet is deemed to have said and done, or tacitly approved or disapproved. Much of this is learned indirectly simply by being born and bred in a Muslim society, but devout Muslims study hadiths so as to be better equipped to emulate the Prophet in every aspect of their lives.

Modern Scepticism about the Hadiths

Many non-Muslim scholars and Muslim modernists are sceptical about the hadiths, and dismiss the bulk of them as inauthentic. They note that in the early period hadiths were rarely cited to establish points of law, and that in the second half of the eighth century, when they began to be cited for this purpose, they were often given with incomplete *isnads*. From this, they infer that the early lawyers relied primarily on individual reasoning; that recourse to the alleged rulings of the Companions came later; and that stress on the importance of Prophetic hadiths came later still. In their opinion, the *Risala* of Shafii (d. 820), the founder of one of the four Sunni law schools, marked the turning point. Before this seminal work was written, Muslims generally assumed that the quranic exhortations to obey the Messenger were addressed primarily to Muhammad's contemporaries and applied to specific situations during his lifetime. Shafii, however, was concerned to draw up a strict hierarchy of sources of law, and therefore marshalled these texts as proof that the Quran itself indicated that the Hadith should be regarded as authoritative. Once Shafii's view gained wide acceptance, definitive Hadith collections were compiled and more attention was paid to *isnads*. The sceptics therefore conclude that, in all probability, many of the hadiths were fabricated in the eighth and ninth centuries by lawyers who wanted to justify their own views by tracing them back to the time of the Prophet.

It is arguable that scholars who take this line have overstated their case. For one thing, they ignore the evidence that Companions and Successors compiled collections of hadiths for their private use. Moreover, they too readily assume that the failure of early Muslim lawyers to cite relevant hadiths in support of specific arguments necessarily implies that these hadiths did not yet exist. Similarly, when they infer from the incomplete *isnads* in works like the *Muwatta* of Malik Ibn Anas (d. 795), that these *isnads* were artfully improved in subsequent generations, they go beyond the evidence. Lawyers who cite authorities that are widely acknowledged often do so obliquely without going into unnecessary detail, and Malik may have done the same. Nevertheless, more recent research, employing different methods, has shown fairly conclusively that the majority of the *isnads* in the standard Hadith collections are suspect. There are many more collections than the three mentioned in the previous section and they overlap to a considerable extent. In some instances, by searching through all the available collections one can find as many as a dozen *isnads* in support of single *matn*. Having done this, the next step is to draw all the *isnads* in diagrammatic form on a single piece of paper so as to show how they are interrelated. The end result looks like a rather spidery tree in which the compilers of the Hadith collections correspond to the tips of the branches, the Prophet is at the base of the trunk, and the intermediate transmitters occur at various points in-between. What is striking is that, when this is done, the tree almost invariably has a trunk. That is to say, most *hadiths* have a single line of transmission for the first two or three generations and then begin to branch out. Now although it is highly likely that some of the things which the Prophet said were heard by only one Companion, it is difficult to believe that the Companion transmitted the saying to only one Successor, and that the Successor in turn transmitted it to only one of his pupils, but that from then on the number of transmitters increased from generation to generation. It is hard to avoid the conclusion that the person whose name occurs at the top of the trunk, at the point where the tree begins to branch, either invented the hadith, or at very least invented that part of the *isnad* which traces it back to the Prophet.

Traditional Biographies of the Prophet

The earliest and most famous of the traditional biographies are *The Life of the Messenger of God* by Muhammad Ibn Ishaq (d. 768) revised by Ibn Hisham (d. 828 or 833), and *The Book of Raiding Campaigns* by al-Waqidi (d. 823). Although these works draw on earlier traditions, they were written more than a century and a half after the events which they purport to describe and cannot therefore be taken at face value. Much of the information which Ibn Ishaq furnishes about Muhammad's early life smacks of legend. For example, he relates that when Muhammad's mother Amina was pregnant with him, she saw a light come forth from her by which she could see the castles of Busra in Syria; and that when as boy he accompanied his uncle with a merchant caravan, they were given hospitality in Busra by a Christian monk called Bahira, who recognised the seal of prophethood between his shoulders. Miracles also abound in Ibn Ishaq's account of Muhammad's ministry in Mecca. These include extravagant details about his night journey and heavenly ascent, which will be mentioned later. We are on somewhat firmer ground with the Medinan period, because the Arabs were accustomed to recording the valiant deeds of their tribal heroes and would therefore have found it natural to preserve similar traditions about the raiding campaigns undertaken by Muhammad and his Companions.

Muhammad's Alleged Moral Failings

In the world-view of medieval Christians, there was no place for a prophet after Jesus. He had been sent as the Messiah in fulfilment of the Old Testament prophecies and was expected to return shortly for the Last Judgement. Moreover, he had warned his followers that before his return false prophets would appear, who would seek to lead people astray. It therefore went without saying that Muhammad must be a false prophet. Thus when, from the mid-twelfth century onwards, genuine information about him came into the hands of Europeans, they almost invariably interpreted it negatively. For example, they learned that Muhammad's first wife, Khadija, was a rich widow much older than him, who had employed him to trade with her goods in Syria. However, whereas Ibn Ishaq had seen this as evidence that Muhammad was extremely trustworthy, Christian writers saw in it the sure proof that he was an opportunist who married for money. They repeatedly made three other allegations which were much more serious than this, namely that he was a fraud who pretended to receive revelations, a lecher who indulged his base instincts, and a warmonger driven by an insatiable appetite for booty. As these allegations are often heard even today, we must examine each of them in turn.

Medieval writers who allege that the Prophet was a **fraud** often suggest that he learned the 'revelations' from the monk Bahira, who was, they assume, a Christian heretic. In view of the obviously legendary nature of the Bahira story, the suggestion does not merit serious consideration. We should note, however, that some of the Prophet's contemporaries insinuated that he relied on an informer and that the Quran itself rebuts this accusation on the grounds that the person they referred to was a foreigner, whereas the revelations were in clear Arabic (16.103). Although there is no substance to the accusations of fraud, the claim that the Qur'an was revealed verbatim by the angel Gabriel needs to be interpreted in the light of the conventions of Jewish and Christian apocalyptic. Similarly, the reference to its preexistence in the guarded 'tablet' (Arabic *lawh*) has to be understood against the background of the widespread ancient-near-eastern belief in heavenly books. For instance, according to the Bible, Moses ascended a mountain to bring down the commandments which God had inscribed on tablets (Hebrew *luhoth*, singular *luah*).

The accusation of **lechery** arose largely because of Christian revulsion at the Muslim practice of polygamy. The facts as far as we can tell are as follows. Muhammad's marriage to his first wife, Khadija, was monogamous and lasted for 24 years until her death left him a widower at the age of 49. He then married Sawda, the widow of one of his companions. After emigrating to Medina he married nine other women. Apart from Ayesha, who was a young girl, most of them were widows of his Companions or of enemies killed in battle, and he seems to have married them primarily in order to give them protection. For political reasons, he also took two concubines: Mariya, a Coptic Christian given him by the Byzantine governor of Egypt, and Rayhana, a Jewess who was a prisoner of war. It is, however, his marriage to Zaynab, the divorced wife of his adopted son Zayd, which furnished the most fuel for anti-Muslim polemic, for it appears that Zayd divorced her so that the Prophet could marry her. The incident is alluded to in the Quran (33.37) but it is open to more than one interpretation. Muslim apologists point out that the Prophet had arranged the marriage between Zayd and Zaynab for political reasons and that they had never been happy together. They argue that Muhammad was opposed to a divorce because he did not want it to come to light that he had been responsible for the unsuccessful match, but that after the divorce God gave her to him in marriage in order to establish an important social reform, the abolition of adoption. Some Muslim modernists, while being careful to affirm that there was no impropriety in the Prophet's relationship with Zaynab, have no qualms in asserting that their falling in love with each other caused the breakdown in her marriage with Zayd. For them, the fact that the Quran was revealed to a man who was not immune to human weaknesses is part of the miracle of Islam.

In view of the Crusades, which were a bloodthirsty and largely unprovoked act of aggression perpetrated by Christians against Muslims living in Palestine, there is more than a touch of irony in the accusation of **warmongering** levelled against Muhammad by Christian polemicists. When persecution in Mecca forced him and his Companions to emigrate to Medina, they had to leave most of their possessions behind. Hence, their subsequent attacks on Meccan caravans were motivated by the desire to compensate for their losses. Nevertheless, there is one incident that arguably casts a shadow over the Medinan period: the massacre of the Jewish clan of the Banu Qurayza and the confiscation of their property. Muslim sources state that between 600 and 900 men were decapitated. We should note, however, that these figures are not given in the Quran. It does not mention the clan by name but simply says 'a group you killed and a group you made captives' (33.26f). There is no way of telling whether or not the numbers have been exaggerated but it is clear is that the incident was provoked by Jewish treachery during the siege of Medina, and not by Muslim bloodlust and greed.

Muslim Veneration of Muhammad

It would be difficult to exaggerate the love, respect and devotion which all true Muslims feel for the Prophet. Because they hold that he is the perfect model for human behaviour, they generally deem him to have been sinless. Consequently, they maintain that when he prayed for forgiveness he did so in order to set a good example for his followers. Moreover, although the Quran stresses that none can intercede with God without God's permission (2.255), they believe on the basis of several hadiths that Muhammad will be permitted to intercede for his community on the Day of Judgement, and that this is what the Quran means when it speaks of him being raised to a station of praise and glory (17.79).

Muhammad's birthplace in Mecca was turned into a mosque in the eighth century. However, his birthday or *mawlid* was first celebrated in 1207 in Iraq. Its celebration was condemned as an innovation by Ibn Taymiya (d. 1328) but it became immensely popular in the late Middle Ages and is observed today in many parts of the Muslim world despite the disapproval of the Wahhabis and other puritanical groups. On his birthday, the Prophet is eulogized in songs and narrations which stress the miracles attributed to him by Ibn Ishaq and other biographers; there are processions and festivities; and food is distributed to the poor.

Of the many miraculous events that are believed to have occurred during the Prophet's life, none fires the popular imagination of Muslims more than the night journey and ascension (*miraj*). According to the Quran, God 'caused His servant to travel by night from the inviolable place of worship to the most distant place of worship' (17.1). It is possible to construe this as a spiritual experience but it is traditionally held that it refers to a physical journey in which Gabriel took Muhammad on a winged mule from Mecca to the temple mount in Jerusalem, whence he ascended through the seven heavens into God's presence before being returned to his bed before morning.

Some even speculate that for the night journey and ascension to have been possible, the Prophet's body must have been made of pure light. This accords with the Sufi interpretation of other passages of the Quran. As one aya speaks of Muhammad as a 'shining lamp' (*sirajan munir an* 33.46), early Sufi commentators meditating on the celebrated light verse (24.35) concluded that he was the mysterious 'lamp' (*misbah*) through which the divine light is shed abroad. Then Sahl at-Tustari (d. 896), commenting on this same aya, alleged that although God is inaccessible light, He gave rise to the light of Muhammad in pre-eternity, and that this light of Muhammad was a luminous mass of adoration in God's presence, from which He subsequently created all the prophets.

Prophets, Messengers, Imams and Saints

According to a well-known tradition, Muhammad stated that God had sent 124,000 prophets and 313 messengers into the world. Islamic theologians maintain that a prophet (Arabic *nabi*) is merely charged with announcing the coming judgement, whereas a messenger (Arabic *rasul*) is in addition sent to promulgate the divine law. Hence, every messenger is a prophet, but not every prophet is a messenger. Although all orthodox Muslims believe that there can be no prophet or messenger after Muhammad, they disagree as to whether or not this rules out the possibility of subsequent revelation. The majority Sunni position is that Islam as a religion was perfected in the time of Muhammad (cp. 5.3). The Shia, on the other hand, believe that

Muhammad was succeeded by a series of infallible Imams, beginning with his cousin and son-in-law Ali, all of whom embody the light of Muhammad. They hold that because most of the Companions of the Prophet erred in accepting the Caliphates of Abu Bakr, Umar and Uthman, their testimony is unreliable. Shiites therefore reject many of the hadiths transmitted by the Companions and prefer their own collections of traditions about the words and deeds of the Prophet and the Imams. The function of the Imams was not to bring new legislation but rather to guide men towards God and to preserve and explain the divine law by bringing out its inner meaning. Nevertheless, the living Imam is held to be the Lord of the Age and the supreme leader of the community. In the Sunni world, many of the Sufis hold not dissimilar views about the saints or 'friends' of God. They believe that a saint may receive revelations which throw light on the inner meaning of the Quran and Hadith, and that in every age there is one saint in particular who is the 'pole' or 'axis' (*qutb*), the leader of the spiritual hierachy. Moreover in many Sufi *tariqas*, the chain (*silsila*) of spiritual leaders linking the present sheikh with his predecessors, is traced back to Ali.

8 Ritual prayer

Introduction

The *shahada* is the first pillar of Islam. By pronouncing it in Arabic, and in the presence of witnesses, a person becomes a Muslim. However, this simple act of testifying that 'there is no god but God and that Muhammad is the Messenger of God' has far-reaching implications. We saw in the previous chapter that a 'messenger' (Arabic *rasul*) is a special type of prophet who is sent to promulgate the divine law. Hence, it has traditionally been held that anyone who publically acknowledges Muhammad as the Messenger of God implicitly undertakes to observe the Sharia, beginning with the performance of the ritual prayer which is regarded as the second of the five pillars.

Prayer in the Quran

Ritual prayer, or *salat* as it is called in Arabic, is mentioned over eighty times in the Qur'an. It is said that it was practised and encouraged by earlier prophets including Abraham (14.40), Ishmael (19.55), Moses (20.14), and Jesus (19.31). However, the generations who followed them neglected it (19.59), with the result that by the time of Muhammad the 'prayer' offered by the Arabs at the Kaaba in Mecca was 'nothing but whistling and clapping' (8.35). The prayer performed by him and his followers was very different and met with opposition almost immediately (96.9f). It involved recitation (96.1, 17.78) and various postures including bowing and prostrating (48.29, 77.48). There are Meccan suras in which the Prophet is instructed to pray at the beginning and end of the day and to observe nocturnal vigils (11.114, 73.1–8). What are probably two Medinan additions to Meccan surahs impose on his followers the duty of glorifying God morning and evening (30.17) and exempt him and them from night vigils (73.20). Another exhorts him somewhat cryptically

> Celebrate the praises of thy Lord before the rising of the sun and before its setting as well as part of the hours of the night and at the sides (or extremities?) of the day (20.130).

An early Medinan sura refers to the 'midmost' (midday or late afternoon?) prayer (2.238). The same sura mentions that when the Jews of Medina became increasingly hostile to Islam, the Muslims were ordered to pray in the direction of the Kaaba to indicate that they were a distinct community (2. 143f). Relatively late Medinan revelations describe prayer as being at designated times (4.103); give instructions concerning ablutions (5.6); and mention the Friday congregational prayers (62.9).

The Prayer Times

According to tradition, the number of daily prayers was fixed in the Meccan period, during the Prophet's *miraj* or ascension, which occurred on the night when he was transported from Mecca to Jerusalem. At first, he received the command that he and his people were to pray fifty times a day. However, Moses (with whom he conversed on his ascent through the heavens) warned him that this would prove too arduous, so Muhammad pleaded with God until the number was eventually reduced to five. They are:

1 the *fajr* or dawn prayer, which may be offered at any time between the break of dawn and sunrise;
2 the *zuhr* or midday prayer, which may be offered at any time between the beginning of the sun's decline from its zenith and the point when an object's shadow becomes the length of the object itself;

3 the *asr* or late afternoon prayer, which may be offered at any
  time from the point when an object's shadow becomes the
  length of the object until just before sunset;
4 the *maghrib* or sunset prayer, which may be offered at any
  time after sunset until daylight ends;
5 the *isha* or night prayer, which may be offered at any time
  between the disappearance of the twilight and the onset of
  dawn, although it is preferable to offer it before midnight.

The Shia often combine the second prayer with the third, and the
fourth with the fifth, so that in practice they say their prayers
only three times a day.

Because the prayer times are determined by the position of the
sun, they vary with the seasons. In Muslim countries, they are
announced daily in the newspapers but elsewhere mosques issue
monthly tables. Moreover, Muslim members of the jet-set often
carry computerised watches and travelling clocks which can be
adjusted to give the correct prayer times in any clime and any
season. This tends to obscure the fact that the principle behind
the set times is very simple and relatively flexible. There is no
need for a sundial, let alone a computerised watch. It is sufficient
to be aware of the approximate position of the sun and to take
care not to pray when it is just rising, is at its zenith, or is just
setting – for to do so might give the impression that the sun itself
was the object of worship.

The Call to Prayer

In Muslim countries, the arrival of the prayer time is announced
by the *adhan*, or call to prayer, which is broadcast from the
minaret of every mosque:

> *Allahu akbar, Allahu akbar. . . .*
> God is most great, God is most great; God is most great,
> God is most great. I testify that there is no god but God. I
> testify that there is no God but God. I testify that
> Muhammad is the Messenger of God. I testify that
> Muhammad is the Messenger of God. Hasten to prayer.
> Hasten to prayer. Hasten to prosperity. Hasten to prosperity.

[Prayer is better than sleep. Prayer is better than sleep.] God is most great, God is most great. There is no god but God.

The longer form, which includes the words enclosed in brackets, is used only for the dawn prayer, and then only by Sunnis. The Shiite *adhan* has two additional clauses: 'Come to the best of actions' and 'Ali is the Wali of God'. The latter clause, they also add to the *shahada*.

The person who gives the *adhan* is known as the muezzin. In the time of the Prophet, this important role was fulfilled by Bilal, a freed Abyssinian slave. On hearing the *adhan*, Muslims repeat it to themselves, except that instead of the clauses which begin 'Hasten to. . .' they say in Arabic, 'There is neither power nor strength save in God.'

Preparation for Salat

Salat (or *namaz* as it is called by Iranians and Muslims from the Indian subcontinent) may be performed in any clean place. If you travel in Muslim countries you will see people praying in fields, in the desert, at airports and railway stations, or by the roadside. If they are praying alone, you will notice that they have placed an object in front of them – perhaps a stick or an item of clothing. This is called a *sutra* and serves to mark off their prayer space as well as to indicate the direction of Mecca. There is no harm in walking in front of a Muslim while he is praying provided that you do not pass between him and his *sutra*. Sunni Muslims usually pray on a mat but Shiites prefer the bare earth.

In addition to finding a suitable place for prayer, a Muslim must be appropriately dressed. A man's clothing should cover his shoulders and the area between the navel and the knees. According to some authorities his head should also be covered. A woman must cover her whole body apart from her face and hands. Men and women alike remove their shoes.

Before performing *salat*, Muslims must be in a state of ritual purity. If they have had sexual intercourse, or a seminal emission (or in the case of women, if they have just completed menstruation, or have given birth in the last forty days) they are required to perform *ghusl*, the ritual washing of the whole body. *Ghusl* is also the norm before the Friday congregational prayers. Otherwise, it is sufficient to perform *wudu*, or ablution. This entails washing the hands, mouth, nose, face, forearms, head and feet in accordance with a set procedure which differs slightly depending on which law school one follows. Many Muslims brush their teeth with a tooth stick, a practice which the Prophet commended. If water is scarce, *tayyamum*, or dry ablution, is performed instead of *wudu*. This entails placing the hands on clean earth, sand or stone, and then blowing off the dust before wiping the face and forearms with them.

Performance of Salat

The basic unit of *salat* is called a *raka*. It comprises a sequence of movements – standing upright, bowing from the waist, standing upright again, prostrating, sitting on the left heel, prostrating again, and then returning to the sitting position – accompanied by quranic recitations and the utterance of set expressions in Arabic. The number of obligatory *rakas* varies according to the time of day: two at dawn and three after sunset, but four at noon, in the late afternoon and at night. This is the minimum. Devout Muslims usually perform additional *rakas*, some of which they consider compulsory because offered by the Prophet, and others which are optional.

The postures adopted in the course of *salat* vary slightly from one law school to another and are often the subject of heated debate. The differences are, however, so minimal that Twelver Shiites and followers of all four Sunni law schools can pray in unison behind the same imam, and regularly do so in Mecca and Medina.

There are also slight variations in the Quranic recitations and formulaic prayers. The following description is not complete but should be sufficient to convey to non-Muslims an impression of what is involved. The *fatiha* (the first sura of the Quran) must be recited in the standing position of each *raka*. In the first two *rakas*, it is followed by three or more ayas from another sura. The transition from one posture to the next is marked by the utterance of the words *Allahu akbar* ('God is most great'). While bowing from the waist, the worshipper says at least three times under his breath 'Glory be to my Lord the mighty' and while prostrating 'Glory be to my Lord the most high'. In the sitting position at the end of the second *raka*, he calls down blessings on the Prophet and makes a testimony of faith which is slightly more elaborate than the *shahada*. In the sitting position at the end of the last *raka*, he repeats the testimony of faith and then says

> O God, send grace and honour on Muhammad and the family of Muhammad as you sent grace and honour on Abraham and the family of Abraham. Surely you are praiseworthy, majestic.

This is repeated with the word 'bless' substituted for 'send grace and honour'. Then he says one or more *duas* (supplications for himself and his family) before concluding by turning his head first to the right and then to the left with the words

> Peace be upon you and the mercy of God.

Praying together, the Friday Congregational Prayer and the Mosque

It is a religious obligation for all Muslims to perform the ritual prayer every day at the five set times. They may pray alone but a strongly encouraged to pray in company of other Muslims. According to a hadith, 'Prayer performed in company is twenty-seven times better than prayer performed by yourself' When Muslims pray together, they choose someone to act as imam, or prayer leader. He should normally be the eldest or the one who is best able to recite the Quran. He requires a *sutra* but is considered to act as *sutra* for those praying behind him.

On Fridays at midday, all free adult males must attend the congregational, or *juma* prayer. Women are permitted to attend but may pray at home if they prefer. (This is the Sunni position. For Shiites, attendance is not obligatory, even for men, although it is strongly encouraged). The *juma* prayer comprises an Arabic sermon or *khutba*, followed by two *rakas* said behind the imam. While waiting for the *khutba* to begin, and again after the two prescribed *rakas*, the worshippers perform additional *rakas* in their own time. The *khutba* has a set structure. It must include praise of God, a credal statement, blessings on the Prophet, prayers for the Muslim community, a Quranic recitation and an exhortation to piety. There is a brief pause in the middle of it, during which the preacher sits down.

The English word 'mosque' is derived from the Arabic *masjid*, which means a place for prostration. According to a hadith, the whole earth is a mosque except for bath-houses and camel pens. Hence, even the *juma* prayer may be performed in a room used for other purposes during the rest of the week. In fact, the Prophet's mosque in Medina was a simple mud-brick enclosure in which he used to conduct all his business. It was open to the sky, except for two makeshift porticos, north and south, supported by palm trunks. One of these served to shelter worshippers from the sun and the other was the home of poor Meccans who had emigrated with him. He himself had no quarters of his own but would spend the nights with his wives who had simple apartments built against the outside of the east wall. Soon after his death, however, Muslims began to build mosques to serve exclusively as places of worship, and within a century the distinction was made between the small *masjid*, which was for everyday use, and the larger *jami* (congregational mosque) which was required for the Friday prayers. The style of mosques has changed down through the ages, and there is still considerable regional variation. The direction of prayer or *qibla* was originally indicated by a whole wall, which sometimes bore a painted mark to identify it. Now the wall usually has an ornate convex niche called a *mihrab*, a feature which was introduced in 706 by the Umayyad Caliph al-Walid I during restorations to the Prophet's mosque in Medina. To the right of the *mihrab*, there is a many-stepped pulpit or *minbar*. The Prophet is said to have had a very simple one which resembled a rustic throne. The early Caliphs and provincial governors had more elaborate *minbars* constructed as symbols of their authority, but they did not become an essential item of mosque furniture until the late Umayyad period. Although a few Umayyad mosques had towers, minarets were first constructed by the Abbasids; in the time of the Prophet the call to prayer had been given from the highest roof in the neighbourhood. Purpose-built mosques have a balcony for women, or a space reserved for them at the rear or to one side.

Prayer on Special Occasions

There are only two festivals which are recognised as such by all Muslims. They are *Id al-Fitr*, which marks the end of Ramadan, and *Id al-Adha*, which coincides with the climax of the pilgrimage. On those days, additional prayers are offered in the morning when the sun is clearly visible above the horizon. They are not preceded by the *adhan*. They comprise two *rakas* followed by a *khutba*. The *rakas* are identical with those performed at other times except that they include additional *takbirs* (repetitions of *Allahu akbar*). Weather permitting, the *Id* prayers should be performed in the open air.

The funeral prayer differs from all others in that it is said standing. It begins with a *takbir* which is followed by recitation of the *fatiha*. After a second *takbir*, the worshippers call down blessings on the Prophet in silence. After a third, they pray in their hearts for the deceased usually using one of several *duas* which request God's forgiveness. The prayer ends with a fourth *takbir* and the turning of the head to the right and then the left with the utterance of the usual formula.

The normal rules for prayer are relaxed somewhat in times of danger (2.239, 4.102). In times of drought, Muslims are expected to pray two *rakas* outside in the open and to include special *duas* for rain.

The 'Barelwi' Litany in Honour of the Prophet

In many mosques in the Indian subcontinent, the *juma* prayer is followed by a litany in praise of the Prophet, which was composed by Ahmad Reza Khan Barelwi (1858–1921). Wahhabis and Muslims from the reformist tradition of Deoband claim that this as an 'innovation' (*bida*) – which is tantamount to saying that it is heretical – and speak disparagingly of Ahmad Reza Khan's followers as 'Barelwis'. They themselves hold that they are Sunni Muslims who adhere to the Hanafi law school, and they object to being thought of as comprising a distinct denomination or sect. In their view, Ahmad Reza Khan was simply seeking to preserve and reform the devotional aspects of traditional Islam as practised in rural India. There is a measure of truth in this in so far as the litany enshrines the age-old Sufi belief in 'the light of

Muhammad'. Shortage of space prevents me from giving the litany in full but the following extracts should convey an impression of what it is like. Led by a cantor, the faithful sing the Prophet's praises in Urdu referring to him by his traditional name of Mustafa ('the Chosen One')

> Hundreds of Thousands of blessings be upon Mustafa, the essence of the mercy of God. Hundreds of thousands of blessings be upon the lamp of the company of prophets. O sinful people, disobedient ones, seize hold of the skirts of the Prophet and follow him.

They greet him in Arabic

> O Prophet of God, peace be upon you.
> O Messenger of God, peace be upon you.
> O Beloved of God, peace be upon you.
> The Benedictions of God be upon you.

And they pray

> O God grant us to love you, to love the Holy Prophet, to love those who are righteous and to love good deeds.
> O God keep us to perform the pilgrimage to Mecca and to visit the Prophet in Medina, and grant us his intercession on the day of Judgement.

The Origins of Salat

Arabic is a semitic language, a member of the same family as Hebrew (the language of the Jewish Bible), Aramaic (the language of the Talmud and Rabbinic Judaism) and Syriac (the language of oriental Christians). These languages have many words in common. For example 'sun' in Arabic is *shams*, which is virtually the same as the Hebrew *shemesh* and the Aramaic and Syriac *shemsha*. No one imagines that the Arabs lacked a word for the sun until Jews or Christians came along and taught them one; it is much more likely that the resemblances between *shams, shemesh* and *shamsha* stem from their derivation from a common ancestor, just as resemblances between French, Italian and Spanish are often to be explained by their derivation from Latin. With specifically religious vocabulary, however, the situation is somewhat different, because the Quran implies that the beliefs and practices enjoined on the Muslims in Muhammad's time were substantially the same as those observed by Jesus and other prophets who were sent to the Children of Israel. Therefore, we cannot ignore the fact that the word *salat* resembles the Aramaic and Syriac *ts^{e}lutha*. It was almost certainly learned from the Jews or Christians, although it may already have entered the Arabic language in pre-Islamic times.

Much more controversial is the origin of the Islamic ritual. According to tradition, the angel Gabriel showed Muhammad how to perform both the prayers and the ablutions which precede them. Moreover, as mentioned earlier, the number of prayers is said to have been fixed at five already in the Meccan period. The evidence of the Quran, on the other hand, seems to point to a more gradual development. In Mecca, Muhammad probably prayed in the morning and the evening, which was the normal Christian practice. In addition he engaged in night vigils like Christian monks and anchorites. The wearing of a cloak (73.1, 74.1) may also indicate a link with Christian asceticism. The word Quran (Arabic *quran* 'recitation'), which denotes the revelations which he received and which he recited liturgically (17.78), resembles the Syriac *qeryana*, the term for a scriptural reading in a church service. Unfortunately, we know all too little about Christianity in the Arabian Peninsula in the seventh century, but there are eyewitness accounts of how St. Simeon Stylites (d. 459), who lived on a pillar near Aleppo, used to stand reciting prayers and psalms and would frequently pause to prostrate himself. Several of the set expressions which accompany the Muslim prayer postures may have originated in the Meccan period and have been inspired by the biblical psalms. For example *Allahu akbar* (God is most great) should perhaps be traced back to the injunction to 'magnify the Lord' (*Psalm* 43.3 etc. cp. *Quran* 74.3).

When Muhammad arrived in Medina, where a third of the population were Jews, daily midday prayers were probably instituted in accordance with Jewish practice, and night vigils were discontinued. It was perhaps at that time too that the Muslims began like the Jews to pray facing Jerusalem, although according to some traditions this had been the norm in Mecca. Soon, however, a further development took place: the Muslims broke with the Jews and were ordered henceforth to pray facing in the direction of the Kaaba, thereby indicating that they were a distinct community. Some scholars have conjectured that the final pattern of five daily prayers was arrived at still later, possibly under the influence of Zoroastrianism.

According to a hadith, God ordained that the congregational prayers should be on Friday because that was the day on which He created Adam, and Adam's first act had been to worship Him. However, the Jews and Christians moved the prayers to Saturday and Sunday respectively; hence only the Muslims worship God in accordance with His original intention. This tradition implies an awareness of the biblical account of the creation, which stipulates that God created Man on the sixth day, the day before the Sabbath. (see *Genesis* 1.26–2.3). The Prophet may well have chosen Friday in order to distinguish the Muslims from the Jews and Christians, and have given this as his rationale. It is clear from the Quran, however, that Friday is not meant to be a day of rest like the Jewish Sabbath or the Christian Sunday, for the believers are explicitly permitted to disperse through the land seeking God's bounty after attending the prayers (62.9f). Moreover there was another reason for choosing Friday: it was market-day in Medina and the city would have been full of visitors. Furthermore, there is evidence that the pagan Arabs regarded Friday as sacred to the goddess Venus, in which case the Prophet would have had good grounds for wishing to give it a different religious orientation. The division of the Friday sermon, or *khutba*, into two halves is something of a mystery. Some non-Muslim scholars have suggested that this was a relatively late development based on Byzantine court ritual. A more plausible explanation is that the *khutba* has two halves because it replaces two *rakas* of prayer (the normal midday prayer comprises four *rakas* whereas on Friday there are only two).

The Purpose and Significance of Ritual Prayer

According to a well-known hadith, the value of an action depends on a person's intention. This is a fundamental principle in Islam, and prevents the lives of Muslims from degenerating into a series of meaningless formalities. Before performing ablutions, they express in their hearts their intention of acquiring purity. Similarly, before performing *salat*, they stand facing the *qibla*, silently reflecting on the specific prayer they are about to offer, and express their intention of performing the prescribed number of *rakas* solely for God. The need to be in a state of ritual purity before *salat* has the effect of making Muslims conscious of God throughout the day and night, even though (Fridays excepted) the ablutions and prayers themselves may occupy as little as forty minutes in every twenty-four hours.

By offering the prayers at the prescribed times, the believers conform to the will of the Creator as observable in His creation, for we read in the Quran

The sun and moon follow a reckoned course
The herbs and trees prostrate themselves.

(55.5f)

And

To God prostrate themselves all that are in the heavens and the earth, willingly or unwillingly, as do their shadows in the mornings and the evenings.

(13.15)

The call to prayer, heard from the minaret, serves as a reminder of the summons which all will hear on the Day of Resurrection. *Wudu* likewise has an eschatological dimension because, according to a hadith, the Prophet said that at the Resurrection his people would be recognised by the bright marks on their foreheads, the traces of their ablutions, and that they should therefore strive here and now to increase the size of those marks. The various prayer postures, and the words which accompany them, express different aspects of the worshipper's relationship with his Lord. In the standing position, he is conscious that he will stand before Him at the judgement, because in the *fatiha* which is recited at the beginning of every *raka*, God is referred to as 'Master of the Day of Recompense' (1.4). However, the subsequent recitation of an additional quranic passage can also be an act of communion and empowerment, because the worshipper feels that he is in a sense in the place of the Prophet, hearing God address him intimately as 'thou' and entrusting him with a message which he must communicate to others. When bowing from the waist, and even more so when pressing his forehead to the ground in prostration, the worshipper expresses his total submission and adoration. When sitting with the palms of his hands turned upward for the final petitions and intercessions (dua), he waits quietly and expectantly on God. Then, as he turns his head slowly to the right and the left he is conscious of his fellow Muslims, all of them equal before God, as well as of the angels on either side of him who keep a record of his deeds.

Praise, adoration, petition and intercession all have an obvious place in the prayer ritual. Penitence does not, although many Muslims ask God's forgiveness as part of the dua and follow the practice of the Prophet in repeating 'I ask God's forgiveness' on completing salat. Moreover, according to a hadith, the Prophet asked his Companions

'If one of you had a river right by his door and he bathed in it five times a day, do you think that there would be any dirt left on him?' They replied, 'No, not a trace.' He said, 'That is how it is with the five prayers; by means of them God wipes away all sins.'

(Robinson The Sayings of Muhammad p. 18)

In addition to its profound religious significance, salat ensures that Muslims take regular exercise. While expressing his adoration of God through a series of physical acts, the worshipper builds up his stamina, strengthens the musculature of his spine, and keeps his joints supple. The final act of turning the head slowly to the right and then to the left releases the tension in the neck and helps prevent arthritis. Moreover, the observance of prayer times which are determined by the position of the sun attunes the worship to the natural diurnal cycle.

We saw above that prayer performed in company is regarded as much more meritorious than prayer performed alone. One reason for this, although I have never heard it expressed in quite that way, is that communal prayer functions as a form of military drill. Women who attend the mosque are usually in a minority and are hidden away at the back, or to one side. Communal prayer is thus a predominantly male activity. When delivering the *khutba*, the imam holds a wooden sword as a symbol of his authority. When he performs the *rakas*, the worshippers move in unison behind him. Great stress is put on their correct positioning. They stand, each man with his feet almost touching those of his neighbour, in long straight lines which run parallel to the *qibla* wall. Anyone who perceives a gap in the line in front of him must move forward to fill it, much as a soldier might be expected to close rank in battle. In fact Surah 61, which chides the believers for their lack of discipline at the Battle of Uhud, affirms that

> God loves those who fight in His way in ranks as though they were a solid wall.
>
> (61.4)

It is thus hard to escape the conclusion that discipline in the mosque was originally intended to ensure discipline on the battlefield.

Ritual Prayer in the Modern World

Salat arguably provides a much-needed remedy for this society of ours in which people have become obsessed with frenetic activity. There is much to be said for finding time during the day to tidy your room, adjust your clothing, wash your body and purify your soul. Moreover, the physical exercise which *salat* entails is as relevant to the sedentary office worker as it was to Arab merchants and bedouin in Muhammad's time. Nevertheless, in other respects the regulations concerning *salat* are problematic. The Prophet lived in the tropics, where it makes sense to rise before dawn and complete the bulk of your work before midday when the weather becomes too hot. The dawn prayer ensures an early start, and the scheduling of the remaining four prayer times between noon and midnight prevents them from interfering with the task in hand. It is questionable whether this pattern is the best for people living in more temperate regions. Moreover, whereas in the tropics the number of daylight hours is relatively constant, nearer the poles there is considerable seasonal variation. In Leeds and Washington, Muslims cope with this as best as they can, but in the north of Scandinavia, where there is virtually no night in midsummer and virtually no sunlight in mid-winter, they solve the problem by observing the prayer times which are operative in Mecca. Another problem is caused by the use of Arabic. There are three strong arguments for retaining this: it exposes the faithful to the inimitable qualities of the Arabic Quran, it ensures historical continuity, and it maintains the unity of the world-wide Muslim community. Nor should one exaggerate the difficulties faced by non-Arab Muslims: the prayer postures are the primary element in *salat*, and the simple formulae which accompany them are soon mastered. Nevertheless, the Arabic *khutba* is usually largely unintelligible to non-Arabs. Many mosques therefore have an address in the vernacular before the *khutba*. The latter then becomes a formality: a liturgical set-piece which is recited from memory week after week and has no relevance to the local situation.

9 Zakat

Introduction

The third pillar of Islam is *zakat*. The word itself originally simply meant 'purity' but it is now the technical term for the Muslim's obligatory annual donation of a fixed percentage of his or her surplus wealth. It is variously translated as 'poor due', 'compulsory charity' or 'obligatory alms tax'. This institution should be seen in the context of Islam's stress on the fundamental importance of charitable giving. In the Quran, the god-fearing are defined as those who

> believe in the Unseen, establish the ritual prayer and expend of that which We have bestowed upon them. . . .
>
> (2.3)

Later in the same sura we read

> They ask thee what they should expend, say, 'The surplus!'
>
> (2.219)

Moreover, according to a hadith, the Prophet said that he would not wish to have a heap of gold as big as Mount Uhud unless he could spend it all in Allah's cause bar the last three dinars. Hence the duty to give generously and in accordance with one's means does not stop with *zakat*. Voluntary almsgiving over and above *zakat* is strongly encouraged; it is known as *sadaqa*.

Zakat in the Quran

The Arabic word *zakat* occurs in the Quran 32 times. In two passages (18.81, 19.13) it has its primary sense of 'purity'. In four others, all of them probably revealed relatively late in the Meccan period, it evidently denotes some form of religious payment which was regarded as an obligation by the prophets of old: Ishmael is said to have enjoined prayer and *zakat* on his family (19.55); God inspired Isaac and Jacob 'to do good deeds, establish prayer and give *zakat*' (21.73); in the time of Moses, God promised a reward in this world and the hereafter for the god-fearing who gave *zakat* (7.156); and the infant Jesus said that God had enjoined prayer and *zakat* on him as long as he lived (19.31). The remaining passages are Medinan. One of them mentions that God imposed prayer and *zakat* on the Children of Israel as part of his covenant with them (2.83). The others all refer to the performance of prayer and the giving of *zakat* as duties incumbent on Muslims (e.g. 5.12) – duties from which not even the Prophet's wives were exempt (33.33). Sura 9, which was revealed towards the end of the Prophet's life, stipulates that if the pagans repent, establish prayer and pay *zakat*, the Muslims should cease hostilities against them (9.5,11).

The Payment of Zakat

The Quran is more explicit about *sadaqa* than *zakat* but the commentators argue that what is says about the former also applies to the latter. The key passage is 2.261–278. God will reward those who expend their wealth in his cause by repaying them many times over in the hereafter. Nevertheless, although the believers are encouraged to 'loan' their wealth to God, God is not dependent on it in any way, because he is self-sufficient. The believers may give openly but it is better to give in secret. Moreover, they should beware lest they nullify their giving by following it up with continual reminders of their generosity. Another passage, 9.60, mentions eight categories of person who are eligible to receive *sadaqa*. They are the poor, the destitute, those employed to collect the funds, those whose hearts are to be reconciled, captives to obtain their freedom, debtors, those engaged in holy war, and wayfarers. The traditional interpretation of the phrase 'those whose hearts are to be reconciled' (al-muallafati qulubuhum) is that it refers exclusively to the inhabitants of Mecca, who had formerly been hostile to Islam but converted en masse when the city was conquered. However, Mawdudi argues that it is justifiable to use zakat funds to calm those who are engaged in hostile activity against Islam or to pay stipends to non-Muslims to gain their support.

From the Hadith, we learn that zakat is payable annually on gold and silver, livestock, and crops, by all Muslims whose accumulated wealth exceeds a basic level called the nisab. No zakat is payable on less than 20 dinars of gold, 200 dirhams of silver, or five camels. According to some authorities, jewellery which is kept to be worn is also exempt. Of anything accumulated above and beyond this, 2½ percent is to be paid as zakat. It may be paid at any time of the year but most Muslims pay it at the beginning of the month of Rajab or at the start of Ramadan. The amount payable on crops is 10%, or 5% if the land has to be artificially irrigated, and it should be paid at the time of harvest. Zakat is to be distributed primarily to the poor and needy and should never be given to the rich or one's own dependants. In Shiite law, zakat is only payable on nine commodities: gold, silver, camels, cattle, sheep, wheat, barley dates and grapes. In addition to zakat, however, Shiites pay **khums**. This is one fifth of their earnings after the deduction of their living expenses. It is spent on the family of the Prophet, orphans, the needy, and travellers.

A person who is too poor to pay zakat is still required to act charitably. The Prophet said,

> Avoid Hell by giving charity, even if it means sharing your last date, and, if you have nothing at all, by speaking a kind word.

(Robinson, *The Sayings of Muhammad* p. 25)

And, according to the Quran,

> Kind words and forgiving of faults are better than *sadaqa* followed by injury.

(2.263)

On one occasion, some of the poorer Companions complained to the Prophet that the rich were carrying off all the rewards because in addition to establishing prayer and observing the fast they were able to give *sadaqa*. He replied that God had prescribed a course whereby even they could give *sadaqa*, because every act of praise, every declaration of the glory of God, and every lawful act of sexual intercourse was a voluntary act of charity.

The Origins of Zakat

According to tradition, the payment of *zakat* was not an organised institution during the Meccan period. At that stage, believers gave *zakat* privately to assist the poor and to liberate slaves. Then, during the second year after the emigration to Medina, the Prophet received a revelation in which the payment of *zakat* was explicitly commanded (2.110). He therefore established it as an obligation, fixed the amount to be paid, and organised its collection and distribution. This is entirely plausible as it is consonant with the quranic evidence.

The word *zakat* was probably originally a foreign word. In Aramaic and Syriac, *zakutha* means 'purity' and 'merit' and could easily by extension have been used by the Jews or Christians of Arabia to denote 'alms'. The Arabic word for voluntary charity, *sadaqa*, points in a similar direction, despite the attempt of early lexicographers to derive it from the Arabic verb meaning 'to be truthful'. In post-biblical Hebrew, *ts^edaqa* (literally 'righteousness') often means alms, as does the Syriac *zedq^etha*. We may conjecture that in the Meccan period, Muslims were aware of the Jewish and Christian stress on almsgiving, and that like them they saw it as a fundamental religious duty, but that it only became institutionalised in Medina where they were in daily contact with the Jews. It is possible that the Jewish practice of tithing influenced the Prophet's decision to levy a fixed percentage as *zakat*.

The Purpose and Significance of Zakat

Quranic commentators assume that the noun *zakat* is derived from the Arabic verb *zaka* which means 'to be purified'. They therefore understand obligatory almsgiving as purifying the soul of the giver. Whether or not this etymology is valid, it brings us to the heart of the **spiritual significance** of *zakat*. Believers are aware that by giving a fixed percentage of their surplus wealth they are fulfilling an important religious obligation and that in the process they are purifying themselves from their greed and selfishness. In addition *zakat* purifies the person who receives it because it saves him from the humiliation of begging and prevents him from envying the rich. Ideally, it binds giver and receiver together in mutual respect and affection. *Zakat* also has an important **socioeconomic function**. Together with the prohibition of usury, *zakat* discourages the hoarding of capital and stimulates investment in the means of production or merchandise, neither of which is usually regarded as zakatable.

Zakat in the Modern World

During the colonial era, the state-sponsored collection of *zakat* ceased in most parts of the Muslim world. It is widely held, however, that a genuinely Islamic government should organise the collection and distribution of *zakat*, because this comes under the rubric of 'ordering what is right and forbidding what is wrong' (cf. 9.112 etc). In recent years, several Muslim countries have therefore taken measures to put this into effect. For example, in Pakistan, since 1981, individuals and corporations have been liable to pay 2½ percent *zakat* on accumulated wealth in excess of 2,000 rupees (about $200) and this has been deducted directly from bank accounts.

Needless to say, adapting what was originally a levy on surplus gold, silver and livestock to the conditions of modern industrial societies is not without difficulty. Classical Islamic jurisprudence allows the use of analogy in dealing with cases for which there is no direct precedent in the Quran or the Hadith. Nevertheless, on such matters the jurists sometimes differ. For example, should *zakat* be levied on the means of production – factories, machinery and the like? It is widely assumed that these are exempt because they do not constitute capital. However if, as some jurists have argued, livestock are not just capital but are analogous to modern means of production, then industrial plant ought to be zakatable. This is the position taken by the government in the Sudan. There are also differences of opinion about who is entitled to receive *zakat*. The traditional view is that it is for the benefit of Muslims. However, in recent years a number of scholars have argued that the word 'poor' should not be defined narrowly as 'the Muslim poor', and several Islamic relief organisations now make a point of extending help to non-Muslim communities in need. Finally, there are problems about how *zakat* should be collected. The Prophet himself appointed collectors, and the first Caliph, Abu Bakr, is known to have punished defaulters. Nevertheless, many Muslims find it hard to believe that they are offering *zakat* to God as a religious duty when the state deducts it from their bank accounts. The system currently operative in Pakistan inevitably reduces *zakat* to a mere tax and provokes citizens to look for ways of avoiding it. As one businessman put it to me bluntly, they cannot deduct *zakat* from what you hide under your bed. In this context, it is worth remembering how the Prophet treated the Thaqif after the surrender of Taif. He was uncompromising on the issue of monotheism and ordered the destruction of their idol of the goddess al-Lat. Nor was he prepared to relax the requirements of ritual prayer. However, to the consternation of some of the Companions, he initially gave the Thaqif exemption from the payment of *zakat*, on the grounds that they would pay when Islam entered their hearts.

10 Ramadan

Introduction

The fourth pillar of Islam is the fast during Ramadan, the ninth month of the lunar calendar. Throughout this month, Muslims are under obligation to abstain from food, drink and sexual relations every day between dawn and sunset. Some Muslims also fast voluntarily on *Ashura*, the tenth day of Muharram. Additional voluntary fasts may be undertaken on other days as well. Moreover, as we shall see below, the Quran prescribes fasting as a means of expiation for various sins.

Ramadan and Fasting in the Quran

The only Meccan passage to mention fasting is 19.26. There we read that Mary was told after the birth of Jesus that if she met anyone, she was to say that she could not speak because she had vowed a 'fast' (*sawm*) to the All-merciful. It is possible that this reflects knowledge of the Christian practice of keeping silence while fasting. However, as Mary had previously been ordered to eat and drink, it seems more likely that in this context the word 'fast' should be interpreted figuratively as abstention from conversation.

The principal Medinan passage about fasting is 2.183–7. As we shall have cause to refer back to it later, it is translated here in full

(183) O you who believe, fasting is prescribed for you, as it was for those before you, that you may fear God. (184) [Fast]

a certain number of days but for him among you who is sick or on a journey, an equal number of other days; and for those who can afford it, a ransom by feeding a poor man. Yet he who voluntarily does good, it is better for him; that you fast is better for you, if only you knew. (185) Ramadan is the month in which the Quran was sent down as a guidance to humankind, explanations of guidance and the criterion. Therefore whoever among you witnesses the moon, let him fast, but whoever is sick or on a journey, an equal number of other days. God desires ease for you, not hardship. Complete therefore the full number of days and proclaim 'God is most great', for He has guided you that you may give thanks. (186) When My servants ask thee concerning Me, certainly I am near. I answer the prayers of the suppliant when he calls on Me. Let them therefore answer My call and believe in Me, that they may be rightly-guided. (187) It has been made lawful for you on the night of the fast, to have intimate relations with your wives. They are garments for you and you are garments for them. God knows that you were defrauding yourselves, but He has turned towards you and forgiven you. Draw near to them now, therefore, and earnestly desire that which God has prescribed for you. Eat and drink until you can distinguish the white thread from the black thread at dawn, then complete the fast until night. Do not have intimate relations with your wives during the period when you are on retreat in the mosques. These are the prescribed bounds of God; do not approach them. Thus God manifests his signs to humankind, that they may fear Him.

In addition, there are five passages which prescribe fasts of various lengths as an expiation for specific sins or as a ransom in lieu of performing various religious obligations (2.196; 4.92; 5.89; 5.95 & 58.4). Finally, 33.35 states that men who fast and women who fast will receive forgiveness from God and a vast reward.

The Observance of Ramadan

The Islamic year comprises twelve lunar months of 29 or 30 days which begin and end at sunset. When the sun sets on the twenty-ninth day of Shaban, the month preceding Ramadan, Muslims look eagerly for the thin crescent of the new moon. If a single reliable witness tells the *qadi* (Islamic judge) that he has seen the moon, Ramadan is deemed to have begun and the faithful are informed that they must commence the fast the following morning. If, however, the sky is obscured by clouds, Ramadan will begin twenty-four hours later. The same process takes place on the twenty-ninth of Ramadan. Thus Ramadan may have 29 or 30 days and it is impossible to tell in advance precisely when it will begin or end. Moreover, as the lunar year comprises only 355 days, Ramadan's position relative to the solar year regresses by about 11 days per annum. In 1998 it will commence around December 20; in 1999 around December 9; in 2000 around November 28, and so on.

During Ramadan, Muslims usually have a light meal before daybreak as recommended by the Prophet. The day's fasting begins when you can 'distinguish the white thread from the black thread at dawn' (2.187). There is a hadith which helps clarify the meaning of this aya

Adiyy b. Hatim said, 'When the aya '. . .until you can distinguish the white thread from the black thread. . .' was revealed, I went and took a white cord and a black cord and put them beneath my pillow. During the night, I looked at them and was unable to distinguish between them. Early in the morning, I went and found the Messenger of God and told him. He replied, "The two threads are the blackness of the night and the whiteness of the day."'

(Robinson *The Sayings of Muhammad* p. 29)

At the end of the night, when the sun reaches 18 degrees below the horizon, there is a false dawn which takes the form of a vertical beam of light in the east. This gives way at the true dawn to a horizontal line of white light stretched across the horizon like a white thread in contrast to the blackness of the night above it. When this appears, the *adhan* is sounded for the dawn prayer and the fast begins.

In Muslim countries, the pace of life often slows down considerably in Ramadan. During the daytime, many shops and businesses are open for shorter hours; some are closed altogether. The devout spend much of their time reading the Quran or engaging in *dhikr*. Others simply sleep. The level of observance of the fast varies from country to country. In Saudi Arabia and Iran, nobody eats, drinks or smokes in public – not even children under the age of puberty, pregnant women, the sick, and travellers, all of whom are exempt from fasting. Similarly, in the tight-knit Muslim communities in the north of England, public infringement of the fast is almost unheard of. In Turkey and Egypt, on the other hand, there is a marked difference between the cities, where some restaurants are open and many people follow their normal routine, and the rural areas, where observance tends to be much stricter.

The fast ends each day at sunset. There is no merit in abstaining from food and drink longer than necessary. The devout therefore break their fast by sipping a glass of water and chewing a few dates before performing the *maghrib* prayer. Then they return home for a full meal. Throughout the evening, towns are animated, shops and restaurants are open, and there is a joyous atmosphere of festivity. The worshippers return to the mosque for the *isha* prayer. This is followed almost immediately by twenty additional *rakas* known as *tarawih*, during which the Quran is recited at length. It is a widespread practice to recite a thirtieth or more of the Quran each night so that it is recited from beginning to end in the course of the month.

During the last ten days of Ramadan, Muslims are encouraged to retreat to the mosques in order to devote their time to the remembrance of God. It is this practice, known as *itikaf*, which is alluded to in 2.187. Those on retreat leave the mosque only to satisfy their basic needs; they are expected to refrain from sexual relations. Mosque attendance for the *isha* and *tarawih* prayers also increases in the last third of the month despite the fact that the latter are not considered compulsory. There is a hadith which exhorts Muslims to search for the Night of Power (*lailat al-qadr*) – the night which the Quran describes as 'better than a thousand months' (97.3) – among the odd-numbered nights of the last ten nights in Ramadan. Although nobody knows its precise date, it is conventionally commemorated on the 27th. On this night, children from the Quran class sometimes attend the mosque to give a public recitation of what they have learned during the previous year, and pious adults often continue their devotions until dawn.

At the first sighting of the crescent moon heralding the arrival of the month of Shawwal, Muslims repeat the words 'God is most great' as decreed in 2.186. The month of fasting is over and the festivities of *Id al-Fitr* begin. These generally continue for three or four days. Shops are closed and people dress up to visit friends and relatives. Gifts are often exchanged and children usually wear brand new clothes. In countries not influenced by Wahhabism, many families visit the tombs of their deceased relatives at this time. The *Id* prayers were described in Chapter 8. Before attending them, each adult Muslim gives two kilograms of flour as *sadaqa*.

The Origins of Ramadan

The name Ramadan is Arabic and means 'scorcher'. In pre-Islamic Arabia, when the Arabs operated with a luni-solar year, it was the midsummer month. As such it was held especially sacred. However, no evidence has survived concerning ritual activity connected with it although we know that it was a time for settling debts and disputes. On the other hand, *sawm*, the Arabic term for 'fast', may be a loan word, for it resembles the Syriac *sawma* and the Hebrew and Aramaic *tsom*. As with *salat* and *zakat*, this suggests the possible influence of Christianity or Judaism. When expounding the words 'fasting is prescribed for you, as it was for those before you' (2.183), some commentators cite a tradition to the effect that the first Christians were ordered to fast in Ramadan, but that finding this too arduous they moved the fast to the spring and extended it by twenty days as a penance for what they had done. This tradition reflects a vague awareness of the difference between Ramadan and the Christian Lent but it can hardly be historically accurate. More credence should be given to reports that the Muslim regulations concerning fasting were modified several times. After arriving in Medina, Muhammad ordered his followers to fast on *Ashura* – the Jewish Day of Atonement (Tishri 10 in the Jewish calendar). Shortly afterwards, *Ashura* was identified with the tenth of Muharram (the first month of the Muslim year). Then, after the break with the Jews, the obligatory month-long fast of Ramadan was instituted and the observance of *Ashura* became optional. At first, the Muslims observed Ramadan by beginning to fast and to abstain from sexual relations as soon as they awoke from sleep. When this proved too much of a strain, 2.187 was revealed encouraging eating, drinking and conjugal relations throughout the night. Finally, shortly before the Prophet died he received a revelation which abolished the lunisolar calendar and replaced it with a purely lunar one (9.36f see Appendix 2). This had the effect of making Ramadan migrate through the seasons as it does now.

With the exception of the final abolition of the lunisolar calendar, the series of changes outlined above seems to be reflected in 2.183–7. We need to remember that Muhammad delivered the quranic revelations to his followers piecemeal and by word of mouth. It would have been relatively easy for him to insert later additions which he claimed that the angel Gabriel had brought him on subsequent occasions, but much more difficult to excise material which had become engraved on people's memories. It is therefore highly probable that some suras contain sequences comprising ayas which were revealed on different occasions. In the present instance we may conjecture that the material was revealed in three successive stages:

1 183–4 prescribed fasting on the Jewish day of Atonement. The reference to 'days' probably implies that the Muslims also fasted in the period leading up to it. Alternatively, in addition to Ashura they may have fasted on the first three days of every month as some traditions suggest.
2 185–6 was added instituting the fast of Ramadan.
3 187 was added to make clear that fasting should not begin before dawn.

Nevertheless, many commentators maintain that all five ayas refer to Ramadan and that they were revealed on a single occasion.

The Purpose and Significance of Ramadan

The observance of Ramadan is extremely rich in meaning. As stated in 2.185, **Ramadan is the month in which the Quran was**

sent down. This is usually interpreted as a reference to the onset of revelation on the Night of Power. According to tradition, although only five ayas, 96.1–5, were communicated to the Prophet on that night, the whole Quran was nevertheless sent down to the nearest heaven in readiness to be revealed piecemeal over the following 23 years. The custom of retreating to the mosques during the last ten days of the month is linked with the fact that the Prophet received the first revelation when on retreat in a cave on Mount Hira on the outskirts of Mecca. That of reciting the Quran from beginning to end in the course of the month is likewise based on the Prophet's own practice. Thus Ramadan is first and foremost a commemoration of the divine revelation.

We have seen that before the month-long fast of Ramadan was instituted, the Muslims fasted on Ashura, the Jewish Day of Atonement. **When Ramadan came to overshadow Ashura in importance, it took on some of the characteristics of the latter.** According to a well-known hadith, the person who observes Ramadan properly will have all his past sins forgiven. According to another,

> When Ramadan arrives, Heaven's gates are opened, Hell's gates are closed, and the demons are chained up.
>
> (Robinson *The Sayings of Muhammad* p. 28)

Moreover, the Jews believe that God is closer to them on the Day of Atonement than on any other day. Similarly, in the course of the quranic legislation concerning Ramadan, God makes a dramatic first-person-singular intervention to assert his nearness to his servants (2.187). The Jewish Day of Atonement occurs nine days after *Rosh Hashana*, the Jewish New Year. According to the rabbis, on this day books are opened in Heaven and judgement is passed on everyone on the basis of their deeds which are inscribed in them. Hence, Jews everywhere greet each other with the words, 'May you be inscribed and sealed for a good year.' Islam has its own structural homologue to this in the night of Shaban 15, which occurs in the middle of the month preceding Ramadan. For it is widely believed that the lotus tree at the extremity of Paradise (53.14) has as many leaves on it as there are people; that it is shaken on this night; and that those whose names are inscribed on the leaves which fall will die within the coming year.

For most Muslims, however, atonement now plays a relatively minor role in their understanding of Ramadan. For them, what is far more important is **the moral and spiritual significance of fasting**. If you merely observe the outward requirements of the fast you will simply succeed in making yourself hungry and thirsty. For this reason, the Prophet stated that it is pointless giving up food and drink unless you also abstain from speaking and practising falsehood. He also said that the fast is annulled by lying, backbiting, ungodly oaths and lustful glances. Hence, in Ramadan devout Muslims strive to control their passions and live better lives. For the Sufis, however, there is a third still higher level of fasting. For them, the ultimate aim is to abstain from attachment to the world so as to focus the thoughts exclusively on God. In the 'two joys' of Ramadan, the daily breaking of the fast and the sighting of the new moon of the Id, they see pointers to the believer's joy at seeing Paradise after death, and the even greater joy of the beatific vision on the Day of Resurrection.

In addition, **Ramadan is of socio-religious significance**. The method and timing of the fast distinguishes Muslims from Jews and Christians, marking them off as a distinct community. The fact that all Muslims fast during the same period and break the fast at the same time increases their sense of solidarity with each other at both the local and the international level. Those who fast become more sensitive to the needs of those who habitually go hungry, and they make a conscious effort to alleviate their plight. Moreover, fasting is a means of curbing antisocial desires. It is not without reason that the quranic teaching about Ramadan is embedded in a longer section which contains communal legislation. In fact the aya which comes immediately after it runs

Do not devour your property among yourselves in vanity, nor seek by it to gain the hearing of the judges that you may knowingly devour a portion of the property of others wrongfully.

(2.188)

The Arabic word translated 'devour' literally means 'eat'. Its metaphorical use in this context serves to emphasize the link between these instructions and those about Ramadan. The message is clear: human beings are inclined to squander their own resources and to be driven by rapacious greed; Ramadan is the first step towards remedying the situation, because it helps the believers control their carnal appetites.

Finally, **Ramadan prepares people for physical privation**. The first day of fasting is always hard and may cause a headache and dizziness. By the second or third day, however, the body becomes accustomed to the new regime and usually functions surprisingly well. Those who have had this experience year by year are less frightened at the prospect of drought than might otherwise be the case because they know that they can survive without eating and drinking for hours on end. This was undoubtedly a great advantage in seventh-century Arabia, where food and drink were often in short supply, especially during the hot summer months.

Ramadan in the Modern World

Ramadan has retained much of its significance and value despite the dramatic changes which have occurred in most societies during the past two hundred years. Nevertheless, the complexity of modern life makes observing the fast problematic for many people. Should bus drivers and airline pilots abstain from food and drink when working? And what of doctors, surgeons, and machine-tool operators? The list is almost endless. The problem is particularly acute for those who perform these jobs in non-Muslim societies, where no allowance is made for the fact that they are fasting. Many Muslims side-step the issue by timing their holiday to coincide with Ramadan but this is not possible for everyone; think for example of students sitting exams or the lecturers who have to mark them. Others take a more pragmatic approach; they fast as best they can but have a light snack or cup of coffee when they fear that their ability to function properly would otherwise be impaired. Unfortunately, they receive little help or encouragement from the *ulama*, most of whom continue to stress that even a minor infringement, like swallowing spittle when cleaning your teeth, is sufficient to annul the fast.

Three further problems arise for Muslims living in northern Europe and North America. The cause of one of them was mentioned earlier in connection with the ritual prayer, namely the marked seasonal variation in the number of daylight hours. In practice, this means that when Ramadan falls in summer, the fasting period is far longer than it would be in Arabia, but that when it falls in winter it is far shorter. The second problem concerns knowing when to begin and end Ramadan. Because northern skies are often occluded at night, local Muslim communities usually take their cue from religious authorities in Saudi Arabia, Iran or Pakistan, rather than rely on local sightings of the new moon. Unfortunately this often results in different ethnic groups being out of step with each other by twenty-four hours, despite living in the same city. The third problem is also linked with the moon. Against the clear skies of Arabia, the moon is visible night after night, and Muslims watch it wax and wane. They know for example that when there is a full moon they are half way through the month. In northern cities, however, the moon may be visible for as few as two or three days. For their inhabitants, the link between Ramadan and the lunar cycle is thus almost entirely severed.

Before leaving the topic of Ramadan in the modern world, there is one further issue which merits comment: the amount of food consumed during the month. It is evident that, although the Quran encourages Muslims to eat and drink at night-time after breaking the fast, Ramadan was not intended to be a month of feasting, let alone one of eating and drinking to excess. In some Muslim countries, however, it is now not uncommon for more meat and fresh vegetables to be consumed in Ramadan than in all the other months put together. There is thus quite a serious gap between the ideal and the reality.

11 The Pilgrimage

Introduction

The fifth pillar of Islam is the *hajj* or pilgrimage to Mecca. It is an obligation on all free adult Muslims to perform the *hajj* at least once in a lifetime provided that it does not cause financial hardship to their families. The *hajj* comprises a series of rituals performed in and around Mecca. It must be performed during the second week of Dhu l-hijja, the twelfth month of the Muslim year. There is also a lesser pilgrimage known as the *umra*. This is not an obligation and may be performed at any time. After performing *hajj* or *umra* many pilgrims visit the Prophet's mosque in Medina.

The Kaaba and its Environs

The area extending several miles around Mecca is known as the *haram* ('sanctuary', 'sacred precinct'). It includes Muzdalifa, Arafat and Mina. Its boundaries, which are called *miqat*, are clearly marked, and non-Muslims are not allowed inside them. In Mecca itself, there is an enormous mosque *al-masjid al-haram* ('the sacred mosque', 'the inviolable place of worship'). It has been expanded several times to accommodate more and more pilgrims, and it now encloses the two hills Safa and Marwa to the East.

The Kaaba is in the centre of *al-masjid al-haram*. It is an approximately cube-shaped building, whose four corners are orientated towards the four cardinal points. As it now stands, it is 15 metres high, 12 metres long and 10.5 metres wide. The walls are constructed of blue-grey granite blocks but their external surface is covered by the *kiswa*, a black brocaded drape with quranic verses in gold, which is replaced annually. There is a door, two metres above the ground, on the north-east side near the east corner. Set into the east corner, is the black stone (*al-hajar al-aswad*) which is probably a meteorite; it is encased in silver. The part of the wall between the door and the black stone is known as *multazim*. The roof slopes slightly towards the north-west where there is a water-spout, *mizab ar-rahma* (the spout of mercy). On the north-west side there is a low detached semi-circular wall called the *hatim*. It encloses *al-hijr*, which is believed to be the burial place of Hagar and Ishmael. According to tradition, the Prophet was asleep inside the *hatim* when the angel Gabriel awoke him to take him on the night journey and ascension. Opposite the north-east side of the Kaaba is the Zamzam well, and opposite the east corner there is a stone with footprints in it which is known as 'the station of Abraham' (*maqam Ibrahim*).

The Pilgrimage During the Lifetime of the Prophet

The principal quranic passages concerning *hajj* and *umra* were revealed in Medina. It is, however, difficult to date them precisely. Indeed some of them were probably revised to meet changed circumstances. Therefore, before they are examined, a brief account will be given of Muslim involvement in the pilgrimage during the Prophet's lifetime, insofar as this can be deduced from Muslim tradition. The pagan Arabs performed both *hajj* and *umra* in pre-Islamic times and they continued to do so until the Prophet finally forbade them in 631. We do not know for certain when the pilgrimage was given a distinctively Islamic form and rationale but this was probably a gradual process. An early Meccan sura refers to God as 'Lord of this house' (106.3), thereby implicitly linking Him with the Kaaba, and in another, the Prophet is ordered to offer a sacrifice (108.2). Thus, even in the Meccan period, the Muslims may have participated in the pilgrimage while refraining from those elements which they considered to be pagan accretions. However, the first revelations which claim that the pilgrimage was established by Abraham probably date from the time of the break with the Jews in 623 or early in 624. That is to say, they are roughly contemporary with the change in the direction of prayer, the institutionalisation of *zakat*, and the institution of the month-long fast of Ramadan. A little later, in March 624, the Muslims plundered a Meccan caravan at Badr. As a result of this, Meccan hostility towards them increased and for several years it was extremely difficult even for individual Muslims to perform *hajj* or *umra*. In 628, the Prophet attempted to perform *umra* with a large body of his Companions, but the Meccans forbade them access, fearing that their intentions were hostile. They did, nevertheless, make a treaty with them at al-Hudaybiya, allowing them to return the following year. On concluding the treaty, the Prophet slew his sacrificial animal and shaved his head. His Companions followed suit and made their way back to Medina. In 629, in accordance with the terms of the treaty, the Meccans evacuated the city for three days while the Prophet performed *umra* at the head of nearly 2,000 Muslim pilgrims. He performed *umra* again in 630 about two months after the conquest of Mecca, but the first Muslim *hajj* did not take place until 631. On that occasion, the Prophet put Abu Bakr in charge of the pilgrims and sent Ali to make a proclamation in Mina on the day of sacrifice, declaring that after that year no pagan would be allowed to perform the pilgrimage or go round the Kaaba naked. In 632, the Prophet himself led the *hajj*. This was the first occasion on which it was an exclusively Muslim affair. Because he died less than three months after completing it, it is known as the Farewell Pilgrimage.

Hajj and Umra in the Quran

There are five suras which contain material about the pilgrimage. They will be examined in approximately chronological order.

Sura 2, 'The Cow', contains four passages which explicitly mention the pilgrimage. The first of them (2.124–9) is thought to date from 623 or 624 like the bulk of the sura. It states among other things that Abraham and Ishmael raised the foundations of 'the house' (another name for the Kaaba); that God made it a resort for mankind and a sanctuary; that He ordained that 'the station of Abraham' should be a place of prayer; and that He ordered Abraham and Ishmael to purify the house for those who circumambulate it, stay by it, and bow down prostrating. The second passage (2.158) is said to have been revealed in connection with the *umra* of 629, in which case it must be a late addition to the sura. It is a statement to the effect that Safa and Marwa are among the places God has appointed for sacred rites and that it is therefore no misdemeanour on the part of those who perform *hajj* or *umra* if they circuit them both. We should almost certainly infer from this that some Muslims objected to the practice because it had pagan connotations for them. The third passage (2.189) may date from 623–4. It mentions that one of the functions of the new moon is to determine the time of the *hajj*. The fourth passage (2.196–203) is the longest and most complex, and is almost certainly composite. The beginning of aya 196 – 'Accomplish the *hajj* and the *umra* for God' – may date from the years 623–4, as may ayas 198f and 203. The addition of 197 and 200–202 probably occurred after the battle of Badr, when it was no longer practicable to consider the pilgrimage an obligation. We may infer from these ayas that, despite the danger involved, some Muslims wished to perform the *hajj* for the purpose of trade. The bulk of aya 196 must be relatively late, possibly after Hudaybiya. The whole passage, as it now stands, stipulates that those who perform the *hajj* or *umra* should do so for God; gives instructions for those who intend to perform them but are prevented; asserts that the *hajj* falls during specific months; and forbids pilgrims to engage in sexual activity, wickedness and quarrelling, but permits them to ply their trade. In addition it alludes to some of the rites that are performed, namely hastening back from Arafat; remembering God near 'the sacred monument' (Muzdalifa); pressing on and imploring God's forgiveness; remembering God even more than you [used to] remember your fathers [at Mina]; and praying for success in this world and the hereafter. There are hints that, although the Muslims are lost in the crowd of pilgrims, their rites of remembrance and prayers differ in important respects from those performed by the Arab pagans.

Surah 22 is called 'The Pilgrimage'. Parts of it may be Meccan but the section dealing with the *hajj* (22.25–37) is undoubtedly

Medinan. From the stress on the Abrahamic nature of the rites we should probably infer that, like 2.124–9, the core of this passage was revealed around the time of the break with the Jews. It narrates how God settled Abraham at the site of 'the house', telling him not to associate other gods with Him but to purify it for those who circumambulate it, stand, bow down and prostrate themselves. Abraham was also instructed to proclaim the pilgrimage among humankind. The pilgrims were to come on lean beasts or on foot. On appointed days, they were to mention God's name over some of their livestock before killing them, eating part of the meat, and feeding the poor and needy with the rest. Then they were to attend to their grooming (literally 'make an end of their uncleanness'), fulfil their vows, and circumambulate the ancient house. Ayas 34–7, which allow Muslims to slaughter the sacrificial animals at home rather than going on pilgrimage, date from after Badr. Aya 25, which refers to the unbelievers who block the way to *al-masjid al-haram*, was probably revealed still later, most likely some time between the siege of Medina in 627 and the conquest of Mecca in 630.

Surah 3, 'The Family of Imran', is usually held to have been revealed in the aftermath of the Battle of Uhud which took place in 625. However, the brief passage about the *hajj* (3.96f) must have been revealed before the Battle of Badr in 624 or after the conquest of Mecca in 630. It states that the first 'house' (i.e. place of worship) established for humankind was the one at Becca (= Mecca?); that it is blessed and a guidance for the whole world; that it contains clear signs such as the station of Abraham; that anyone who enters it will be secure; and that pilgrimage to it is a divinely-ordained duty for anyone who can afford it.

Sura 9, 'Repentance', includes the proclamation which Ali was instructed to make at Mina during the *hajj* of 631. It contains three ayas (9.3,18 & 28) which make it clear that pagans are not to be permitted access to the sacred places.

Sura 5, 'The Table Spread', contains two passages (5.1f & 94–97) about the *hajj*. They deal principally with the ban on hunting for those attired as pilgrims. These passages seem to date from the time of the Farewell Pilgrimage of 632, although there is a tradition that 5.94 was revealed immediately after the Treaty of Hudaybiya in 628. Some of the Companions, who were prevented from performing *umra* on that occasion, were apparently sorely tempted by the abundance of game.

Performing the Umra

The *umra* may be performed at any time of year. Before passing the *miqat*, which mark the boundaries of the *haram*, the pilgrims trim their nails and moustaches, remove unnecessary body hair and take a bath. They then adopt *ihram*, the sacred attire. For men, this consists of two seamless white sheets, one (the *izar*) is wrapped round the waist above the navel while the other (the *rida*) covers the shoulders but leaves the head exposed. Women, on the other hand, wear ordinary stitched garments which extend to the wrists and ankles; they should not be veiled but their hair must be concealed. On adopting *ihram*, the pilgrims perform two *rakas* of prayer and begin reciting the *talbiya*:

> *labbayk allahumma labbayk, labbayk. la sharik laka. labbayk. inna l-hamda wa-nimata laka wa-l-mulk. la sharika lak.*
> Doubly at thy service O God, doubly at thy service, doubly at thy service. Thou hast no partner. Doubly at thy service. Surely all praise and all favour are thine, and all dominion. Thou hast no partner.

During the *umra*, pilgrims are not permitted to wear shoes; to comb the hair or beard; to wash with soap; or to use perfume. Moreover, they must abstain from sexual relations; they are forbidden to hunt; and they should not wantonly kill any living creature, or cut or pluck plants.

On reaching Mecca, the pilgrims perform ablutions and then enter *al-masjid al-haram*, preferably through *bab al-umra* ('the gate of visitation'). The men temporarily adjust their *rida* so as expose the right shoulder while circumambulating the Kaaba. Together with the women they make seven circuits in an anticlockwise direction. In the first three circuits some perform what is known as *ramal*, walking briskly while shaking their shoulders like a warrior going bravely into battle. All seven circuits are begun at the eastern corner where the pilgrims kiss or salute the black stone. While circumambulating, they are also permitted to touch the southern (Yemeni) corner with the palms of their hands. There are special Arabic prayers prescribed for each circuit but those who cannot memorise them may humbly beseech God in their own words in any language. The following prayer is especially popular. It is said in each circuit while walking between the Yemeni corner and the eastern corner

Our Lord, give us in this world what is good, and in the hereafter what is good, and guard us from the punishment of the Fire. And cause us to enter Paradise along with those who are devout, O Almighty, O All-forgiving, O Lord of the Worlds.

(Cp. 2.201)

On completing the seventh circuit, the pilgrims attempt to kiss the black stone for the eighth time. Then, with hands raised above their heads, they press their chests and cheeks against *multazim* – the part of the wall between the black stone and the door of the Kaaba – imploring God's mercy and blessing. Finally, they move to *maqam Ibrahim*, ('the Station of Abraham'), and perform two *rakas* of prayer. This completes the ritual of *tawwaf*, or circumambulation.

After praying at or near *maqam Ibrahim*, the pilgrims come to the well of Zamzam and drink three draughts of its water. They then proceed to perform the *sai*, which entails going on foot between the two hills of Safa and Marwa seven times. Women do this at a normal pace but men begin to run when they pass between two green pillars and continue to do so for 800 yards until they pass between two more. The pilgrims recite special prayers from memory, repeat them after their guide, or address God in their own words.

At the completion of the *sai*, the ceremonies of the *umra* are over. The pilgrims therefore have their heads shaven at Marwa and abandon *ihram*.

Performing the Hajj

The *hajj* takes place in **Dhul-Hijja**, the last month of the Muslim year. On the **7th** day of the month, before passing the *miqat*, the

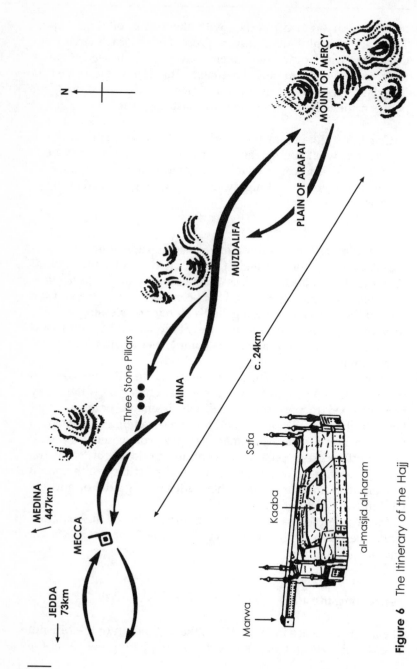

Figure 6 The Itinerary of the Hajj

N

JEDDA
73km

MEDINA
447km

MECCA

Three Stone Pillars

MINA

MUZDALIFA

PLAIN OF ARAFAT

MOUNT OF MERCY

c. 24km

Marwa

Safa

Kaaba

al-masjid al-haram

pilgrims consecrate themselves in the same way as for *umra*. They enter *al-masjid al-haram*, preferably through *bab as-salam* ('the gate of peace') and listen to a sermon describing the rites which they are about to perform. The rites themselves begin on the **8th**. After the dawn prayer, the participants perform *tawwaf* and *sai* as in the *umra*. They then proceed to Mina, which is about three miles from Mecca, where they offer the five daily prayers beginning with the midday prayer on the 8th and ending with the dawn prayer on the **9th**. After sunrise on the 9th, they proceed to the plain of Arafat, which is nine miles further east, repeating *talbiya* and prayers for forgiveness on the way. At Arafat, the guide pitches a tent, either on the plain or, if possible, on the adjacent mountain, Jabal Rahma ('the Mount of Mercy'). The *wuquf* or 'standing' at Arafat is the most important element of the *hajj*. From midday to sunset, the pilgrims stand before God humbly remembering him and asking his forgiveness; a second sermon is preached, and the midday and late afternoon prayers are combined and performed behind the imam. At sunset, the tents are struck and at a given signal the pilgrims disperse on foot to Muzdalifa repeating *talbiya* and prayers for forgiveness as they go. On arrival, the sunset and late evening prayers are said one after the other, and the night is spent in prayer. On the **10th**, just before sunrise, the pilgrims collect a number of small pebbles the size of date stones. Then, after the dawn prayer, they return to Mina where there are three stone pillars known as *jamrat al-ula*, *jamrat al-wusta* and *jamrat al-aqaba*. Each pilgrim throws seven pebbles at *jamrat al-aqaba*, which is the furthest pillar from Muzdalifa. He uses his right hand and recites with every throw

In the name of God. God is most great. The casting of pebbles is against Satan.

After this, the *talbiya* is no longer to be used. If possible, the pilgrim who can afford to do so proceeds to sacrifice a sheep, a goat or a camel, and has his head shaved. (A woman is not permitted to shave her head; she has about an inch of hair removed instead.) He may now resume his ordinary clothes but may not have sexual intercourse until he has returned to Mecca and performed a further *tawaf* and *sai*, which is normally done on the same day. Then he goes back to Mina. On the **11th**, he may offer the sacrifice and perform *tawwaf* if he was unable to do this the day before. Then between the noon prayer and sunset, he throws pebbles at all three *jamrat* and spends his time in *dhikr* and in asking God's forgiveness. On the **12th**, he remains at Mina. If he has still not managed to offer a sacrifice and perform *tawwaf* he may still do so. Otherwise he repeats the pebble-throwing. On the **13th**, he again throws pebbles at the three pillars and then returns to Mecca. He performs *tawwaf* for the last time, followed by two *rakas* at the Station of Abraham. Finally, he drinks Zamzam water while facing the Kaaba and then departs.

Visiting the Prophet's Mosque in Medina

After performing *hajj* or *umra*, those who can afford it go to Medina, where the Prophet is buried. It is a time-honoured practice to stay there for ten days so as to perform fifty prayers. This is not a religious obligation but it is strongly encouraged. The reason for this is that Medina is the second most holy city in Islam and according to a hadith, prayer in the Prophet's mosque is a thousand times more excellent than prayer in any other mosque apart from *al-masjid al-haram* in Mecca.

Medina is due north of Mecca. Hence the *qibla* is in the south. The Prophet is buried in the south-east corner of the mosque beneath a green dome. According to a hadith, he said

The space between my house and my pulpit is one of the gardens of Paradise.

Visitors therefore make straight for the front of the mosque and try to offer two *rakas* of prayer with the *minbar* on their right and the tomb to their left, in the area known as *riad al-janna* ('the Garden of Paradise'). They then file between the *qibla* wall and the metal grille which shields the tomb. Turning their backs on the *qibla*, they face the grille and imagine themselves face to face with the Prophet, greeting him in silence. Then (if they are Sunnis) they greet Abu Bakr and Umar who are buried with him. On subsequent visits, they attempt to perform *salat* behind each of eight pillars in *riad al-janna*. Between the fixed prayers, they spend much of the time in the mosque reading or reciting the Quran.

The Origins of Hajj and Umra

The Quran implies that the Kaaba was the first place of worship ever built on earth (3.96). According to tradition, it dates from the time of Adam. Hence, the Quran's somewhat ambiguous reference to Abraham and Ishmael having raised its foundations (2.127) is usually interpreted to mean that they rebuilt it after it had fallen into ruin. Most Muslims believe that God revealed the rituals of *hajj* and *umra* to Abraham (cp. 2.128, 22.26–30) but that subsequent generations corrupted them by adding idolatrous practices. Through divinely-given revelation, however, the Prophet Muhammad restored them to their original monotheistic form.

Although there is no reason to doubt the existence of Abraham, he is not a historical figure in the sense that we can locate him accurately in time and space. His story belongs rather to pre-history. There is thus little point in debating whether he really visited Mecca. What I propose to do instead is to discuss the Kaaba and the performance of the *umra* and the *hajj* in pre-Islamic times, in terms of their possible links with paganism and Judaism. Then I will tackle the question of whether Abraham was popularly associated with Mecca before the rise of Islam.

The fact that the four corners of the **Kaaba** point north, south, east and west, and that the black stone is set in the east corner, the direction of the rising sun, suggests that the building may have been linked in some way with a solar cult. There are several other details which lend weight to this theory. In pre-Islamic times the *kiswa* was red, yellow and white (the colours of the rising sun?); the Kaaba had no roof and people were not allowed in it at night (because the worshippers had to be exposed to the sun?); and it was surrounded by 360 idols (the approximate number of days in the solar year?). On the other hand, there is a tradition that the roof was added when the Kaaba was rebuilt after a fire, when the Prophet was still only a youth. Hence, the original purpose of the building may by then have been only partially remembered. Moreover, there are other details which suggest associations with less specific forms of Arab paganism. These include the name 'house' which implies that the Kaaba was thought of as the dwelling place of a deity; the veneration of a stone, probably thought of as representing the deity himself;

reports that there was a well inside the Kaaba into which pilgrims threw votive offerings; and others that the Kaaba contained gold and silver discs representing the sun and moon, a giant statue of the god Hubal, and a wooden dove which was the symbol of Venus. The most plausible explanation of the *hatim* is that it was a pen for the sacrificial animals. The fact that it makes the plan of the Kaaba resemble that of a small church with a semicircular apse facing Jerusalem is probably fortuitous. We should, however, note that according to some reports there was a picture of Mary and Jesus on the inner surface of one of the walls of the Kaaba, and according to others Muhammad adopted Jerusalem as the *qibla* before emigrating to Medina.

Nothing can be deduced from the name of the *umra*, because the word simply means 'visit' or 'visiting'. Whereas the *umra* may now be performed throughout the year, in pre-Islamic times it was performed uniquely in Rajab, the first month of spring. Moreover, the participants sacrificed animals at the Kaaba. This practice was discontinued once the link with spring was severed, but we saw earlier that the Prophet and his Companions took sacrificial animals with them when they set out to perform the *umra* in 628. In Arabia, spring is the time when ewes and goats yean and camels calve. In all probability, the *umra* was originally a spring-time sacrifice performed by the Arab nomads to secure fecundity and prosperity for their flocks. As such, it resembled the Jewish Passover, or rather the ancient Semitic festival on which the Passover was based.

In addition to the sacrifice the pre-Islamic *umra* included a *tawaf* in which the participants circled round the Kaaba naked. Rituals in which worshippers circumambulate an object or building are found in many religions. Usually, however, this is done in a clockwise direction, that is to say the pilgrims imitate the diurnal path of the sun. We may conjecture that this was originally the case with the *umra*. The Muslims continued to begin the *tawwaf* at the east corner (like the rising sun) and to make seven circuits (as does the sun in a the course of a week), but the Prophet ordered the Muslims to cover themselves and to walk round anti-clockwise thereby weakening the link with the solar cult.

The *sai* between Safa and Marwa was also performed in pre-Islamic times but it may have been a separate rite which the

Prophet absorbed into the *umra* and *hajj*. We saw earlier that the Quran indicates that some Muslims were distinctly unhappy about it (2.158). According to tradition, the reason for this was that the Arab pagans used to venerate two idols called Isaf and Naila, the one placed on top of Safa and the other on top of Marwa. Some commentators relate that the Prophet used to perform the *sai* when the idols had been removed and that the aya in question was revealed to reassure a Companion who had not wanted to run between the two hills after seeing the Quraish replace them.

The Arabic word **hajj** is related to the Hebrew *hag*, which is derived from a verb meaning 'to go round' and denotes a pilgrim festival. At the Feast of Tabernacles, one of the three pilgrim festivals celebrated by the Jews, the worshippers circled round the altar seven times on the seventh day. The pre-Islamic *hajj* took place in the autumn and seems to have been linked with Arafat and Mina rather than with Mecca. Arabs from far and wide used to attend fairs at Ukaz, Majanna and Dhu l-Majaz, where they engaged in trade, before proceeding to Arafat to begin the *hajj* rituals. As an autumnal festival, the purpose of the *hajj* was probably to ensure the regeneration of the vegetation after the scorching-hot summer. There is evidence that the deity worshipped at Muzdalifa was a fertilising thunder god known as Quza. Unfortunately, we know nothing about the local deities in Arafat and Mina but it is probably significant that in pre-Islamic times the dispersal to Mina on the 10th used to take place at the moment of sunrise. It has been suggested, therefore, that when the pilgrims stood on Arafat they were engaged in a ritual struggle with the demon of the summer sun, whose powers had already begun to wane. The next day, the demon was chased to Mina at sunrise and then ritually stoned. On the other hand, we should note that going out to stand before God was an important element in the life of ancient Israel (cp. *Exodus* 19.17, 23.17) and Jewish influence cannot therefore be ruled out. There are reports that after the *hajj* rituals the Arabs used to celebrate the noble deeds of their ancestors at Mina, a practice which is alluded to in the Quran where it is superseded by the remembrance of God during the *hajj* itself (2.200).

We have seen that in pre-Islamic times, the *hajj* and *umra* had a number of recognisably pagan elements but that in other respects they resembled well-known Jewish rituals. It would, however, be wrong to jump to the conclusion that the 'Jewish' elements were necessarily the result of Jewish influence, because in some instances Jewish rites seem to have arisen through the reinterpretation and transformation of more ancient pagan practices. For example the Jewish Passover commemorating the deliverance from Egypt is a thinly-disguised pastoral rite of spring. This brings us to the vexed question of whether the Quran restored the *hajj* and *umra* to their pristine monotheistic form, or whether it simply made them respectable by giving them a monotheistic interpretation. Muslims generally take the former view; non-Muslim historians of religion the latter. Rather than entering the lists on one side or the other, I propose to tackle the related question of whether Abraham was linked with Mecca and its environs in pre-Islamic times.

Since the late nineteenth century, a number of non-Muslim scholars have argued that Muhammad invented the Abrahamic link with Mecca during the Medinan period, as a matter of political expediency. They maintain that he did this after the break with the Jews in order to strengthen the case for regarding Islam as an independant religion with a better pedigree than Judaism. They further allege that the Quran contains two different portraits of Abraham. In the Meccan suras, like so many other prophets mentioned in the Quran, Abraham is simply sent to warn his people of impending judgement. In the Medinan suras, on the other hand, he is the ancestor of the Arabs who built the Kaaba; he is prepared to sacrifice his son in obedience to God's command; and he establishes the pilgrimage rites. Those who have taken this line have overstated their case. There are three Meccan suras which contain hints that the full-blown story of Abraham may have been known to members of the Prophet's audience long before he moved to Medina. Sura 90, which begins with an oath by 'this city' (Mecca?), also contains an oath by 'the begetter and he whom he begets' (90.3), which some commentators interpret as a reference to Abraham and the son born to him in his old age; Surah 87 mentions 'the scrolls of Abraham', thus implying that he received revelation (87.19); and Sura 53 says that Abraham 'fulfilled his pledge' (53.37), probably alluding to his willingness to sacrifice his son. Nevertheless, it is a striking fact that there is no evidence that the Arabs ever called their sons Abraham or Ishmael before the rise of Islam. This suggests that those who cherished the belief that Abraham was linked with their city were an insignificant minority. Early Muslim historians mention isolated individuals in Muhammad's time who were monotheists despite being neither Jews nor Christians. They refer to them as 'hanifs', a word used in the Quran of Abraham (3.67 etc., usually translated 'upright' or 'true in faith'). It seems likely that the hanifs favoured an Abrahamic interpretation of at least some of the rituals performed in and around Mecca.

The Purpose and Significance of the Muslim Hajj and Umra

Although some of the pre-Islamic Arabs may have interpreted the rites of *hajj* and *umra* monotheistically and held that they originated with Abraham, it seems likely that the majority probably thought of them as pagan practices which were associated with the sun or with local divinities. Islam retained the pre-Islamic rites in modified form but purged them of all pagan connotations, linking them instead with God's prophets Adam, Abraham and Muhammad, as well as imbuing them with eschatological significance.

The connection with the solar cult was severed in three ways. First, slight modifications were made to some of the rituals: the colour of the *kiswa* was changed, pilgrims were forbidden to go naked, the direction of the *tawwaf* was reversed, and the timing of the dispersal to Mina was altered. Second, other rituals such as standing on Arafat and stoning the pillars at Mina were retained but given new interpretations. Third, the seasonal nature of the rites was abolished by allowing *umra* to be performed at any time of year and by replacing the luni-solar calendar with a lunar one so that the *hajj* season was no longer fixed. The association with local divinities was abolished by purging the sacred sites of idols, and by making the *hajj* begin and end at Mecca thereby bringing all the rituals under the aegis of the one God. Moreover, the Quran explicitly states that God does not require the flesh and blood of animals but rather the piety of those who sacrifice them (22.37). The meat is not given to him but shared with the poor, and eaten.

The traditions linking Adam with the Kaaba and the *hajj* are relatively late. They were probably invented to explain the quranic statement about the 'house' in Becca being the first that was established for humankind (3.96). It is related that when Adam and Eve were expelled from Paradise, Adam alighted on Safa and Eve on Marwa. Adam later complained to God that he no longer heard the voices of the angels, so God instructed him to build a house on earth and to circumambulate it in the way that he had seen the angels circumambulate his throne. According to another version, however, God Himself built the Kaaba before the creation and subsequently sent it down to Adam in a dome of light. There is also a tradition that Gabriel taught Adam how to perform the prayers when he was standing on Jabal ar-Rahma.

The Abrahamic interpretation of the *hajj* is much more firmly rooted in the Quran (2.124–9, 22.25–37). According to tradition, the Kaaba was destroyed during the flood but Abraham rebuilt it on the original site having first ploughed the land to uncover the foundations. He also retrieved the stone from Abu Qubays, a mountain on the outskirts of Mecca, where it had been hidden to keep it safe. At that time, the stone was white but it subsequently became black because of repeatedly being touched by sinners or, according to another account, menstruating women. The Station of Abraham is where Abraham stood summoning humankind to the *hajj*; God caused his footprints to remain there. The *sai* between Safa and Marwa is said to have originated when Hagar went to and fro looking for water to prevent her infant son Ishmael from dying of thirst. The reason why the pilgrims run part of the course is that she ran when she passed through a valley because she could no longer see Ishmael whom she had left seated near the Kaaba. Her prayers were eventually answered when the spring of Zamzam miraculously burst forth beneath Ishmael's hand. When Gabriel was showing Abraham how to perform the various rituals, the Devil appeared so Gabriel ordered Abraham to stone him. This happened three times before the Devil finally withdrew, which is why the pilgrims now stone three pillars. When they arrived at the place now called Arafat, Gabriel asked Abraham whether he knew what he had to do. Abraham replied 'I know' (Arabic *arif*), which is how the place received its name. Finally, the sacrifice at Mina commemorates God's provision of a sacrifice in place of Abraham's son. It is now universally held by Muslims that the son in question was Ishmael but there is evidence that Muslims originally identified him as Isaac, as do Jews and Christians.

Orthodox Muslims believe that the Prophet restored the rites of *hajj* and *umra* to their pure Abrahamic form. Nevertheless, although they do not think of Muhammad's actions as innovations, it is of deep significance to them that the rituals which they perform today are exactly the same as those that he performed on the Farewell Pilgrimage. For example, they uncover their right shoulders before circumambulating the Kaaba because there are hadiths stating that that is what the Prophet did. Performing the *hajj* therefore brings Muslims closer to Muhammad and might almost be thought of as a sacrament of communion with him.

In addition to its Adamic, Abrahamic and Muhammadan resonances, the *hajj* has profound eschatological significance. The pilgrim's longing to see God's house in this world is a preparation for seeing Him face to face in the next. Setting aside provisions for the journey to Mecca reminds him that the only provisions he will take with him to the hereafter are piety and good works. Bidding farewell to his family and friends is a foretaste of being wrenched from them at death. Donning *ihram* reminds him that at the resurrection he will meet God wearing only a seamless shroud. Circumambulating the Kaaba, he thinks of the angels circling God's throne. Touching the black stone, he swears allegiance to God as though he were taking his right hand. Running between Safa and Marwa, his mind turns to the scales at the Last Judgement and he hopes that his good deeds will outweigh the bad. Mingling with the crowds on the plain of Arafat, brings home to him what it will be like on the Day of Resurrection, when a great throng of people which no man can number pour forth from the graves to face the judgement.

Despite the rich layers of religious meaning that the various rituals have for the participants, the *hajj* is (or was) as physically demanding as a military assault course, which must originally have been one of its functions. The fact that during the first three circuits of the *tawwaf* some of pilgrims strut round the Kaaba shaking their shoulders like warriors going into battle seems to bear this out.

When all is said and done, however, some of the rituals seem almost childish and are bound to appear puzzling to Muslims who are totally unaware of their pagan origins. Umar, the second Caliph is said to have had reservations about kissing the black stone and to have declared that he would not have done so if he had not seen the Prophet doing it. Ghazali had similar problems with running between Safa and Marwa, and throwing pebbles at the stone pillars in Mina. His solution was to describe the rituals as 'inexplicable duties' and to suggest that by performing actions 'to which the soul does not readily conform, and whose significance is not easily grasped by the mind' the pilgrim demonstrates 'the perfection of his homage and adoration' (Al-Ghazali *Inner Dimensions of Islamic Worship* pp. 105f.). This is why it is the fifth and final pillar of Islam. Whereas the other four all have a clear rational basis, the *hajj* entails an element of blind obedience; hence the pilgrim's watchword is the *talbiya*: 'Doubly at thy service O God! Doubly at thy service!'

Hajj and Umra in the Modern World

As the result of the discovery of oil in Saudi Arabia in 1938, what was then a minor desert kingdom has become one of the richest countries in the world. The change in Saudi Arabia's economic fortunes, together with the advent of the jet airliner and other safe and rapid methods of transport, has transformed the holy places and the conditions under which they are visited.

Long past are the days when pilgrims had to endure a gruelling month-long camel-ride through the desert not knowing whether they would reach their destination alive. Now the majority fly to Jedda and complete the last leg of the journey by coach. Because the flight-path crosses the *miqat*, some put on *ihram* before boarding the plane. Others change in mid-flight. When it is not the *hajj* season, pilgrims intending to perform the *umra* travel in the same planes as businessmen visiting Saudi Arabia for more mundane purposes. This results in the strange spectacle of male passengers disappearing beneath the video screen, which was showing *Terminator 2* only minutes earlier, and reappearing clad in white sheets. Jedda airport has most modern facilities but pilgrims performing *hajj* are often left stranded outside it for hours on end, waiting beneath aesthetically pleasing but woefully inadequate shelters intended to protect them from the burning sun.

The road from Jedda to Mecca is good but the surface is thin and an unexpected shower of rain can produce massive pot-holes over night. After the *miqat* signalling the boundary of the *haram*, there are signs in Arabic with slogans such as 'God is most Great', 'God be glorified' and 'I ask God for forgiveness'. Unfortunately, they are interspersed with others advertising Seiko watches and Pepsi Cola. There is an even greater shock in store. On the left-hand side, only a two or three hundred metres from *al-masjid al-haram*, there is a large yellow M. This is subliminal advertising at its most crass – Mecca/McDonalds. By now, of course, the pilgrims have their minds set on higher things, for they are busily chanting *labbayk allahumma labbayk*. Alas, on their right they are soon confronted with an advert for Al-Bayk, the Saudi answer to Kentucky Fried Chicken.

For Muslims residing in Jedda, the *umra* can be performed with the minimum of discomfort. They drive into Mecca, park their cars beneath the Hilton Hotel, perform the rituals, and then have a shower before grabbing some fast food and motoring home. Those who are on *hajj*, or who have come for *umra* from further afield, face greater difficulties. The quality of their accommodation will vary considerably depending on how much they can afford to pay. Some book into luxury hotels while others sleep ten to a room without air-conditioning. Guests of the royal family stay in the palace overlooking the inviolable place of worship and can offer the five daily prayers 'behind' the imam without leaving the comfort of their room, although even they must go down and mingle with the throng to perform *tawaf.*

Al-masjid al-haram is awesome in size. In the nineteen-fifties, its area was expanded from 29,127 square metres to 160,168 square metres. It now has an upper storey which is reached by escalators, and it can also accommodate worshippers on the roof. The central courtyard is paved entirely with smooth white marble. There are lines painted on it which radiate from the corners of the Kaaba to help the pilgrims keep track of the number of circuits they have performed and to prompt them to salute the black stone. The *maqam Ibrahim* has been moved further from the Kaaba and is protected by a crystal dome inside a gilded metal-framed glass structure. It appears to have been so worn by generations of pilgrims that all that remains is a stone slab pierced by two holes shaped roughly like the soles of feet. The entrance to the well of Zamzam now looks like a subway on the London underground except that it is larger, cleaner, made of marble, and has a partition down the centre: men enter on the right, women on the left. At the bottom of a broad flight of steps there are extensive facilities for performing ablutions. On the men's side, in the far left-hand corner behind a plate-glass wall, there is a massive pump guarded by a man seated at a desk. The whole mosque is floodlit at night and it is frequented continuously by pilgrims, but those who choose to visit it late in the evening may find that their devotions are interrupted by an army of men in blue boiler suits performing *tawaf* with giant vacuum cleaners.

Because of the increase in the area of the mosque, the two 'hills' Safa and Marwa are now situated inside it. Safa is in the southern corner under a circular dome which is supported by eight pillars. It is an impressive rugged mound about twice the height of a man, and some people still scramble to the top. To reach Marwa, which lies almost due north, the pilgrims pass through a long marble corridor which is air-conditioned and has propeller-like fans suspended from the ceiling. Those who are thirsty may stop to fill a disposable plastic tumbler with Zamzam water from one of the cream-coloured urns which are strategically placed here as elsewhere in the mosque. There are four lanes for two-way traffic: the able-bodied keep to the outside-left while those in wheelchairs race down the centre protected by marble crash barriers. The green pillars indicating when to run have been replaced by green neon lights but there is no longer much of a valley. Moreover, it is now impossible to see the Kaaba even from the top of Safa, which makes it difficult for pilgrims to identify with Hagar's concern to keep an eye on her child. The gentle ascent to Marwa is covered with small white tiles. Nothing remains exposed of the hill itself apart from a few square feet of bare rock protruding two or three inches above its cement surround.

The other sacred sites have likewise been adapted to accommodate the swelling number of participants in the *hajj*.

On the plain of Arafat there are showers the height of lamp-posts to cool them down and signs indicating a centre for lost pilgrims. The Mount of Mercy has steps carved into it, a white obelisk at the top, and notices informing the superstitious that there is no evidence that the Prophet or his Companions used to tie rags or bits of wool to objects in the vicinity. The stone pillars at Mina are situated in what looks like an enormous two-storey car park. On the ground floor, each pillar is surrounded by a low circular wall which serves to catch the pebbles. The pillars themselves soar through holes in the roof and are stoned simultaneously by a second crowd of pilgrims standing on the upper deck. The size of the pilgrim throng causes logistic problems on the day of sacrifice, when approximately 600,000 sheep are slaughtered. The terrain is far too barren to support such large flocks; it would be impractical for that many pilgrims to despatch their own sacrificial animals in the open air; and there are not enough poor people in Saudi Arabia to share the meat. The pilgrims therefore buy tickets for sheep which are imported from Australia, slaughtered for them in an abattoir, quick-frozen, and re-exported to poor Muslim countries.

Unlike Mecca, Medina has not been commercialised. The road approaching the city has signs encouraging pious ejaculations but adverts for consumer goods and fast-foods are conspicuously absent. Like the mosque in Medina, the Prophet's mosque has been drastically altered over the centuries. In his lifetime it was a simple affair of sun-baked mud walls and palm-trunk pillars. Now it is a forest of marble columns with gold capitals, is richly carpeted, and can hold more than a third of a million worshippers. Everywhere there are racks of Qurans, and urns full of Zamzam water brought by road from Mecca in huge tankers. At sunrise the smooth white marble pavement surrounding the mosque shimmers like a sea of crystal. After the prayers, the recently departed are carried out and buried in the nearby cemetery (*jannat al-baqi*, pronounced *bagi* by the Saudis) along with the Companions of the Prophet and many other illustrious Muslims. The Wahhabis have destroyed all the monuments so that the graves are now bare unmarked mounds, but the burial site of the third Caliph, Uthman, is well-known, and Shiite pilgrims bring plans which enable them to locate the graves of the Imams.

Before 1950 the annual number of *hajj* pilgrims from abroad was rarely more than 100,000. Now it is approximately 1,000,000. To these must be added a further three-quarters of a million who come from within Saudi Arabia. For the Saudis, this certainly causes problems but it also brings in an enormous amount of revenue. For other Muslim countries, the effect is potentially devastating. Try to imagine yourself running a third-world economy when every family wishes to slaughter a sheep on Id al-Adha and thousands of people want to withdraw their life-savings and spend them abroad. Most countries have taken measures to ensure that at least some of the pilgrims' expenditure benefits them rather than Saudi Arabia. They allow a fixed number of their citizens to perform the *hajj*; sell them regulation uniforms and travelling bags; and encourage them to travel on their own airlines.

According to a well-known hadith, the person who performs the *hajj* in order to please God, and who behaves correctly throughout its duration, will return home like a newborn child. There is no notion of original sin in Islam. Hence, those who perform the pilgrimage hope to receive forgiveness and to return with their slate wiped clean. Moreover, they believe that God will reward them for patiently bearing the hardships which they encounter. For this reason, Muslims rarely complain about adverse conditions on the *hajj*. In any case, for most of them, seeing the Kaaba and encountering fellow Muslims from all over the world are such overwhelmingly positive experiences that the less pleasant aspects of their visit are soon forgotten. Those are two key elements in the pilgrimage which have not changed. Now, as in the past, pilgrims return believing that they have been blessed by their visit to the House of God and feeling fully integrated into the world-wide community of Muslims. This feeling of integration has always been extremely important, especially for those coming from the margins of the Muslim world: the once remote areas of sub-Saharan Africa and the Far East. The *hajj* takes them out of their syncretistic milieu and brings them into contact with authentic Islam. What has changed, however, since the advent of Wahhabism, is the notion of what that 'authentic' Islam entails.

12 | The Sharia

The Nature and Scope of Islamic Law

The Arabic word *sharia* means a path or an approach to a watering place, but in its technical sense it denotes the law laid down by God. The aim of Islamic jurisprudence or *fiqh* (Arabic 'understanding') is to understand God's law. Throughout the Muslim world, up until the nineteenth century, *fiqh* was the most important academic discipline. It had two principal components: *furu al-fiqh*, the 'branches' of understanding, and *usul al-fiqh*, the 'roots' of understanding. The *furu al-fiqh* comprised the various laws. They were grouped in topics under two main headings: *ibadat*, or acts of worship, namely: purity, prayer, almsgiving, fasting, and pilgrimage, and *muamalat*, or interpersonal acts, including family law, mercantile law, criminal law and so on. The *usul al-fiqh* covered the categories of law (obligatory, recommended, permitted, disliked and forbidden); the sources of law (which varied depending on the school but always included the Quran, the Sunna, and consensus); the rules for extrapolating norms from the sources (rhetorical devices and the use of analogy); and the theory of *ijtihad*, the exercise of independent judgement. The law was implemented by qadis and muftis. The qadi (Arabic *qadi* 'judge') was usually appointed by the political authority and dealt principally with family law, charitable trusts and civil disputes. The mufti was an expert who could give legal rulings or *fatwas*.

The Principal Sunni Law Schools

Although there is a certain amount of legal material in the Quran there is no systematic law code. This should be clear from the last four chapters which have dealt in turn with ritual prayer, *zakat*, fasting and pilgrimage. In each case it has emerged that, although Muslim practice is firmly rooted in the Quran, the Quran by itself gives the believers insufficient guidance on how to fulfil their obligations. We have seen, for example, that there are ayas which stress the importance of prayer, and others which mention certain prayer times or prayer postures, but none which stipulate precisely when and how *salat* should be performed. There are similar problems with the laws which govern interpersonal acts. Take for instance the punishment for theft. The Quran states that the thief's hand should be cut off (5.38) but it leaves many questions unanswered. Does the law apply to children as well as adults? Should it be enforced when the culprit is old, infirm or pregnant? Are there mitigating circumstances such as poverty or feeble-mindedness? Is amputation the punishment for first offenders or merely for habitual thieves? Must the object taken be of value? And what evidence is required to convict someone of theft?

While the Prophet was still alive, the Quran's silence about matters such as these was unproblematic. Sometimes he would receive additional revelations which threw light on difficult questions, but more frequently he gave his own judgement or fell back on the customary law of Medina. After his death, however, the situation changed dramatically. There were no further revelations. Nor, in the view of most Muslims, could there be another charismatic figure like Muhammad who would be a lawgiver in his own right. The first four Caliphs administered justice on the basis of the Quran and the decisions of the Prophet. Like him, they also made a *hoc* decisions of their own and drew on the customary law of Medina. However, these last two elements proved increasingly difficult to justify. In matters of administration, for instance, the third Caliph, Uthman, was severely criticised for reversing the policies of his predecessor. Moreover, as Islam spread further and further afield, it became less and less practical to rely on the customary law of Medina. A decisive development took place in the Umayyad period, when the provincial governors appointed qadis to whom they delegated their judicial authority. The governors reserved the right to judge any case themselves if they so desired, and they could of course dismiss the qadis if they saw fit. Nevertheless, the qadis were in charge of the day-to-day administration of justice. They were, for the most part, devout Muslims who were concerned to proceed in accordance with the Quran and Islamic tradition, but they also drew on local custom and frequently had to use their own discretion. Many of the decisions which they took were incorporated into law. The appointment of qadis who were legal experts led in turn, during the early Abbasid period, to the emergence of distinct law schools (*madhhabs*) in different geographical centres. Only those which are still extant will be mentioned below.

The Hanafi School is named after Abu Hanifa (d. 767), who was a native of Kufa in Iraq. He was an academic lawyer and never served as a qadi. His thought was transmitted by his students, notably Abu Yusuf (d. 798) and Muhammad b. al-Hasan ash-Shaybani (d. 804). The latter should perhaps be regarded as the real founder of the school. The Hanafi school is the most liberal and flexible of the four Sunni schools. In establishing points of law, Abu Hanifa relied in the first instance on the Quran, then on analogical reasoning (*qiyas*). He regarded the latter as more important than tradition although he of course took hadiths into account. A jurist's use of analogical reasoning to extend a quranic ruling to a new case depends on his ability to identify the underlying cause or reason (*illa*) for the original ruling. For example, according to the Quran, after the call has been given for the Friday congregational prayers, it is forbidden to buy or sell goods until the prayers are over (62.9). The underlying reason for this is that buying and selling distract people from praying. Therefore, by analogy, all other transactions are likewise forbidden at this time because they too are a distraction.

Abu Hanifa invoked the principle of 'legal discretion' (Arabic *istihsan*, literally 'approving or deeming something preferable') in order to justify departing from the letter of the law in circumstances where rigidly applying it would lead to unfairness. For example, the Quran requires women to keep their bodies covered when in the presence of men other than their husbands or close relatives (24.31), but Hanafi jurists argue that this rule may be set aside in the case of a woman who is seriously ill and needs a medical examination. The principle of *istihsan* rests, they argue, on the following ayas of the Quran

> Those who listen to the word and follow the best meaning in it, those are the ones whom God has guided, and those are the ones endued with understanding.
>
> (39.18)

> And follow the best of what has been sent down to you from your Lord.
>
> (39.55)

> God intends facility for you, and He does not want to make things difficult for you.
>
> (2.185)

In a similar vein, the Prophet is reported to have said

> The best of your religion is that which brings ease to the people.

Moreover, although the Companions did not explicitly formulate the principle of *istihsan*, there are several well-documented instances of them apparently acting on it intuitively. The most famous example is Umar's decision not to enforce the penalty of amputation for theft during a serious famine.

As well as allowing ample room for the exercise of reason, Abu Hanifa relied on consensus (*ijma*) to establish points of law, because the Prophet said, 'My people will never agree on an error.' He held that only the consensus of the qualified legal authorities of a given generation was absolutely infallible, but in practice Hanifis have often accepted a local consensus, sometimes involving only a handful of jurists. The Hanafi or Kufan school was the dominant law school during the Abbasid Caliphate and subsequently became the official school of the Ottoman Empire. Largely because of this, it has continued to be the most widespread school. It is adhered to by the majority of Muslims in Syria, Jordan, Turkey, North India, Pakistan, China and Central Asia. Approximately a third of all the Muslims in the world are Hanafis.

The Maliki School was founded by Malik b. Anas (d. 796) who was born and died in Medina. The Maliki or Medinan school represents a reaction against the earlier more speculative approaches to law. Malik compiled *al-Muwatta* ('The Trodden Way') which is essentially a legal textbook based on tradition. In dealing with a given topic, he cites the precedent set by the Prophet followed by reports about the opinions and acts of the Companions and later Medinan worthies. Then he discusses them and accepts or rejects them in the light of the legal tradition of Medina and his own reasoning. Let us take for example the *aqiqa*, the sacrifice offered by the parents of a newborn child. Malik first cites a hadith on the authority of a man of the Banu Damra who quoted his father as saying

> The Messenger of God was asked about the *aqiqa*. He said, 'I do not like disobedience (*uquq*)' as if he did not like the name. He said, 'If anyone has a child born to him, and wants to sacrifice for his child, then let him do it.'

Then he cites two reports, which resemble each other but have different isnads, and which relate that the Prophet's daughter Fatima weighed the hair of her children and gave away in *sadaqa* the equivalent weight in silver. According to the first report, she did this for her daughters as well as her sons, whereas the second report mentions only Hasan and Hussein. After this, Malik cites a series of traditions about later Medinan practice: Abdullah b. Umar (the son of the second Caliph) gave a sheep as an *aqiqa* for both his male and female children; al-Harith said that an *aqiqa* was desirable even if it was only a sparrow; Malik himself had heard that there had been an *aqiqa* for Hasan and Hussein; and Ibn az-Zubayr made an *aqiqa* for his male and female children of a sheep each. Finally he gives his own opinion as follows

> What we do about the *aqiqa* is that if someone makes an *aqiqa* for his children he gives a sheep for both male and female. The *aqiqa* is not obligatory but it is desirable to do it, and people continue to come to us about it. If someone makes an *aqiqa* for his children, the same rule applies as with all sacrificial animals – one-eyed, emaciated or sick animals must not be used, and neither the meat or the skin

is to be sold. The bones are broken and some of the family eat the meat and give some of it away as *sadaqa*. The child is not smeared with any of the blood.

It is clear that in the last analysis what counted for Malik was the legal tradition of Medina. In his view, it was this that enshrined the will of the Prophet as understood by the Companions. Thus, whereas Abu Hanifa had understood *ijma* as the consensus of the qualified legal authorities of a given generation, Malik defined it as the consensus of the people of Medina.

Malik is also credited with having favoured the principle of *istislah*, or taking into account the public interest. He held that new laws could be introduced which had no textual basis in the Quran or tradition, provided that they are intended to secure a benefit or prevent a harm and are in harmony with the objectives of the Sharia to protect the five essential values, namely religion, life, intellect, lineage and property. The principle of *istislah* was frequently invoked by rulers who wished to impose taxes or take other measures which might have appeared to be innovations. The Maliki school is no longer favoured in Medina, its place of origin. It is, however, the dominant school in Upper Egypt and North Africa.

The Shafii School was founded by Muhammad b. Idris ash-Shafii (d. 820). His *Risala* ('Treatise'), which was written during the last years of his life when he was living in Cairo, was mentioned in Chapter 7 in connection with modern scepticism about the Hadith. Shafii studied in Mecca, Medina, Iraq and Syria. He was thoroughly acquainted with the various schools of law which existed in his time, but he refused to identify with any one of them. He aimed instead at unifying them by providing a sound theory of the sources from which law is derived. His genius lay in redefining existing terms so as to produce a strict hierarchy of authorities. First and foremost came the Quran. Then he marshalled evidence from the Quran itself to show that Muslims were duty-bound to obey the Prophet because his legal decisions were divinely-inspired. Thus the Sunna as enshrined in the hadiths was the second most important authority. In many people's opinion, however, the hadiths were often contradictory. Shafii therefore devoted much of the *Risala* to demonstrating that apparent contradictions could be explained in terms of a later hadith abrogating an earlier one, or one hadith representing an exception to the rule laid down in another. Next in Shafii's hierarchy of sources came *ijma*, 'consensus'. We have seen that the Hanafis and Malikis both invoked this concept although they disagreed over what was meant by it. Shafii's solution was to redefine it as the agreement of the entire Muslim community, including both legal experts and laymen. In so doing, he paid lip-service to its value while in practice considerably reducing its importance. Shafii's final source of law was analogy (*qiyas*). Because of his emphasis on the Sunna, he left much less scope for this than Abu Hanifa had done. Moreover, *qiyas* was the only form of reasoning that he allowed; he did not approve of *istihsan* or *istislah*. Today, adherents of the Shafii School are found predominantly in Lower Egypt, South India and Malaya.

The Hanbali School is named after Ahmad b. Hanbal (d. 855). He was born and died in Baghdad but travelled extensively in search of hadiths, of which he compiled an enormous collection known as *Musnad al-Imam Ahmad*. He was by temperament more of a traditionist than a jurist and never wrote a book on the theory of *fiqh*. Nevertheless, he did write one in which he gave his opinion about various legal questions. He was a pupil and admirer of Shafii and had an even higher opinion of the Hadith than he did. He insisted that the Quran and the Sunna, as enshrined in sound hadiths, were the primary source of law, and that the texts were to be understood literally. Later Hanbalites recognised four further sources of law ranking them in the following order: *fatwas* of the Companions provided that they do not contradict the Quran or Sunna; the sayings of individual Companions when in conformity with the Quran and the Sunna; traditions with weak isnads; and finally, analogy when absolutely necessary. Ibn Taymiya (d. 1327), whose writings greatly influenced Ibn Abd al-Wahhab (d. 1792), was a Hanbalite. The success of the Wahhabis led ultimately to the recognition of Hanbalism as the official law school in Saudi Arabia and Qatar. It also has many adherents in Iraq and Syria.

The Origins and Development of Twelver Shiite Jurisprudence

The majority of Shiites are known as Ithna-Asharis or Twelvers because they believe that the Prophet was succeeded by a series of twelve Imams. Ali, the Prophet's cousin and son-in-law, was the first Imam, and Hasan and Hussein, Ali's sons by the Prophet's daughter Fatima, were the second and third respectively. As we saw in Chapter 3, Hussein died fighting the troops of Yazid, the Umayyad Caliph, at the Battle of Karbala. This incident had a profound effect on the Shiites, and the subsequent Imams were politically quiescent. Jafar as-Sadiq (d. 765), the sixth in the line, was especially renowned for his learning and piety. The Umayyads left him unmolested in Medina where he had a large circle of students, the majority of whom were Sunnis. Shiites maintain that the circle included the eminent jurists Abu Hanifa and Malik b. Anas, both of whom respected him as a teacher of traditions.

Although the Shiite Imams transmitted traditions orally, no Shiite scholar compiled a written collection of traditions before the Buyid period. The earliest collection is *al-Kafi fi Ilm ad-Din* ('The Sufficient in the Science of Religion') of Muhammad al-Kulayni (d. 940). There are three others which Shiites regard as canonical: one compiled by Ibn Babuya (d. 991) and two compiled by Muhammad at-Tusi (d. 1067). These differ from the Sunni collections in that they include sayings attributed to the Imams as well as prophetic hadiths.

Shiite reflection on the *usul al-fiqh* began in earnest in early eleventh-century Baghdad with scholars who were influenced by the rationalism of Mutazilite theology. A pupil of Ibn Babuya known as Shaikh al-Mufid (d. 1022) accepted the pre-eminence of the Quran and the Shiite traditions but argued that reason should be used to interpret texts which appeared partially contradictory. He defined *ijma* as the consensus of the Islamic community when it corresponded to the opinion of the Imam, and he rejected the use of analogy. Sharif al-Murtada (d. 1024) championed the authority of the traditions but argued that those which were contrary to reason should be rejected, as should those which were transmitted by only one informer. On the other hand, Muhammad b. al-Hasan at-Tusi (d. 1067), who is also known as Shaikh at-Taifa ('Sheikh of the Community'), accepted traditions transmitted by only one informer, provided he was a Shiite.

After the Mongols sacked Baghdad, the town of Hilla on the Euphrates became the chief centre of Shiite scholarship. Allama al-Hilli (d. 1325) was the most distinguished jurist during the

Mongol period. He was also the first Shiite scholar to be styled Ayatollah ('Sign of God'). He argued for the importance of *ijtihad* (the exercise of independent judgement in questions of law) but stressed that this was the prerogative of the ulama. The ordinary believer should follow the decisions of a living authority known as a *mujtahid*. However, as *mujtahids* are fallible human beings, they are free to change their opinion and it is only to be expected that they will disagree among themselves at times.

When the Safavids came to power in 1501 and imposed Twelver Shiism as the state religion of Persia, they imported Shiite ulama from Iraq and elsewhere to instruct the people. As foreigners brought in by the new regime, the ulama were at first very insecure. In the long term, however, the Safavid revolution greatly enhanced their status. By the second half of the seventeenth century, some ulama were claiming that from a Shiite perspective, the real ruler of the country ought to be an infallible *mujtahid*, and that the Shah should deal with temporal affairs as his minister. Extravagant claims of this sort led to increasing antagonism between jurists of two opposing schools of thought: the Akhbaris and the Usulis. On the one hand, the Akhbaris (from Arabic *akhbar* 'reports') entirely rejected *ijtihad*. The only sources of law which they were prepared to accept were the Quran and Sunna as interpreted by the Imams. They regarded all four canonical collections of traditions as reliable and recognised additional traditions including some from Sunni sources. On the other hand, their opponents the Usulis (from Arabic *usul* sources) championed *ijtihad*. They accepted the Quran, the Sunna, consensus and intellect as valid sources. They regarded many of the traditions in the four collections as unreliable, and refused to countenance the use of traditions not transmitted from the Imams by reliable Shiites. Since the beginning of the nineteenth century, the majority of the Shiite ulama have been Usulis. Nevertheless, the Akhbaris are still influential in and around the Iraqi city of Basra and on the island of Bahrain.

'Divinely-specified' Penalties

In the minds of non-Muslims living in Europe or North America, the word Sharia almost invariably conjures up gruesome images of punishment by stoning, amputation or flogging. It should by now be clear that this is a gross distortion, as the Sharia is in fact an all-embracing system which regulates everything from the performance of ritual prayer to the conduct of international relations. Nevertheless, because Islamic modes of punishment loom so large in the western imagination, it is appropriate for them to be discussed here in more detail.

Islamic law distinguishes between *hudud* punishments, which are based on the Quran or Sunna, and are therefore understood to be divinely-specified, and *tazirat* punishments, which are left to the discretion of the judge. The *hudud* punishments are as follows: for theft, amputation of a hand; for fornication, 100 lashes; for adultery, stoning to death; for false accusation of unchastity, 80 lashes; for wine-drinking, 40 lashes according to Imam Shafi but 80 according to the founders of the other law schools; and for banditry, execution, amputation of an arm and a leg on opposite sides of the body, or exile, depending on the seriousness of the crime. The punishments for theft, fornication, and false accusation of unchastity are clearly specified in the Quran (5.38; 24.2; and 24.4 respectively). The punishment for banditry is allegedly based on the Quran (5.33) although it is arguable that the aya in question is not a legal injunction but rather a description of what the unbelievers were doing to each other in the time of the Prophet. The Quran orders the believers to avoid wine (5.90f) but says nothing about flogging wine-drinkers. It seems likely that this particular punishment was first imposed by Umar, although there are hadiths that attribute it to the Prophet. The second Caliph may also have been responsible for the decision to stone adulterers, although he allegedly claimed that he did so on the basis of a quranic aya which was still recited in his day despite not being included in the written text of the Quran.

In traditional Islamic societies, the *hudud* punishments were rarely implemented. Their existence as a theoretical possibility served both as a deterrent and as a reminder of the seriousness with which God viewed antisocial crimes, but because the Prophet asserted that their implementation should be prevented whenever doubt existed, Muslim jurists laid down very strict criteria for their applicability.

Let us take for example the stoning of adulterers. The punishment is not implemented, unless the accused openly confess their guilt or four witnesses testify against them. The difficulty of finding four witnesses to testify against a crime which is usually committed in private is exacerbated by the fact that they run the risk of receiving 80 lashes for false accusation of unchastity if the accused are acquitted. There was a famous case, early in the history of Islam, where this happened. One day, Abu Bakra, a Companion of the Prophet, was sitting on the covered balcony of his house in Basra chatting with three friends, when a gust of wind blew open the shutters of the house across the road and they caught sight of the governor, al-Mughrira b. Shuba, making love to a woman called Umm Jamil. When al-Mughira later left his house to lead the prayers, Abu Bakra prevented him from doing so and accused him of adultery. News of the incident reached the Caliph, who called the governor to account. Al-Mughira protested his innocence, saying that the woman whom they had seen him making love to was none other than his wife. He suggested that the Caliph should interrogate the witnesses and ask them whether they had seen the woman's face. Abu Bakra was the first to be questioned. He claimed to have seen al-Mughira between a woman's thighs, moving in and out like a probe in a jar of eye-shadow. He admitted that he had not seen the woman's face but insisted that he had recognised her feet as those of Umm Jamil. The second and third witnesses gave similar testimonies except that they claimed to have seen the faces of the accused. The fourth witness said that he had seen the woman's feet and naked buttocks and had heard her gasping, but admitted that he had not been able to recognise her. When questioned further, he added that he had not seen al-Mughira move in and out like a probe in a jar of eye-shadow. The Caliph concluded that the first three witnesses had been lying. He therefore had them punished with 80 lashes and set the accused free.

The criteria for imposing the penalty of amputation for the crime of theft vary from society to society but are often even more stringent than those which apply to stoning in cases of alleged adultery. In Pakistan, for example, where amputation has been on the statute books since 1979, it has never been implemented. This is because it is only deemed applicable in cases where the thief believed that the victim was unaware that the crime was taking place; where the stolen property was worth more than $100; where it was stolen from a device intended for its safe-keeping; where there were three eye-witnesses who are sane adult males known to be good Muslims; and where the punishment would not endanger the life of the criminal.

The Sharia in the Modern World

In Chapter 4, we saw that Shah Wali Allah's contemporaries in eighteenth-century Delhi held that for Sunni Muslims 'the door of *ijtihad*' had been closed some eight hundred years earlier, and that he challenged this assumption by citing the works of Ibn Taymiya. Many books on Islam by western writers refer to the closure of the door of *ijtihad* in the course of the tenth century, as if this were an established fact. They assume that from then on jurists could no longer exercise independent judgement and were expected to follow the precedents reached by earlier authorities who belonged to their school. It is now recognised, however, that this is an oversimplification. What is true is that no new law school came into existence after the tenth century and that because of the influence of Shafii the four extant schools had by that time grown closer to each other, adopting what is known as the 'classical' theory of law. They all accepted the fundamental importance of the Quran and Sunna, the need for analogical reasoning, and the validity of consensus defined as the agreement of the qualified legal scholars in a given generation. It is also true that the trauma caused by the Mongol invasions in the mid-thirteenth century led to a widespread tendency for Muslim scholars to be more concerned with preserving and codifying their intellectual heritage than with creative thinking. Moreover, much of the literature produced by Sunni jurists between the tenth century and the nineteenth does give the impression that the Sharia is static and timeless. However, a more attentive reading of the texts shows that this was in many instances a deliberately contrived illusion – an attempt to give the impression that Islam as practised in their day and age was in every respect identical with the Islam of the Prophet and his Companions – and that, despite appearances, they did in fact continue to practise *ijtihad*.

In the nineteenth century, most Muslim countries succumbed to European influence and this had a marked effect on the way in which Islamic law was applied. The Ottomans carried out a number of legal reforms. These included abolishing the *hudud* punishments and replacing them with the French Penal Code, and systematising the Hanafi law of obligations so that it could be enforced uniformly by secular law courts. In those countries which were colonised by Europeans, similar developments took place. Elements of British, French or Dutch law were introduced and the scope of the Sharia was restricted. Moreover, its regulations were simplified and codified so that they could be understood and enforced by European administrators without reference to the classical sources. Meanwhile, modernists including Sayyid Ahmad Khan in India and Muhammad Abduh in Egypt called for a new *ijtihad* which would disregard the established schools.

In the post-colonial period, the majority of Muslim countries have either inherited or adopted a judicious mixture of European and Islamic law. This is equally true of democracies such as Turkey, Pakistan and Bangladesh; absolute monarchies like Morocco; and socialist dictatorships including Egypt, Iraq and Syria. In many instances, however, Muslim governments are under increasing pressure from Islamists to impose the Sharia. This has sometimes led to token Islamization, as for instance in 1983 when President Nimeiri of Sudan introduced the *hudud* punishments without observing the traditional safeguards. Other countries, such as Pakistan, have opted for a gradualist approach. It has a Council for Islamic Ideology which was appointed to bring the existing law into conformity with the Sharia. In the meanwhile, every citizen has the right to approach the Federal Sharia Court to complain that a specific law is repugnant to Islam.

Historically, the Hanafi school has had much more extensive experience of government than either the Hanbali school or the Shiite Usuli school. Unlike them, it has therefore developed a complex network of checks and balances. For this reason, Pakistan is arguably a better role model for Islamization than either Saudi Arabia or Iran. All the same, the reintroduction of the Sharia after the colonial interlude poses formidable problems, even when *ijtihad* is given free rein. Had the Muslim world not been colonised by Europe, Islamic law might have developed in step with society. That was not the case, however, and its natural development was on the contrary artificially arrested. Therefore, Islamicization almost inevitably looks like an attempt to put the clock back. Despite this, very few Muslims have dared openly question whether a return to the Sharia is desirable. Those who have done so include Fazlur Rahman (d. 1988) and Mahmud Muhammad Taha. (d. 1986). Rahman, a Pakistani scholar who lived the last years of his life exiled in Chicago, argued that although the moral claims of the Quran were absolutes, the quranic legislation was historically contingent. Thus, for example, the Quran permitted polygamy and slavery because it would have been unrealistic to abolish them in seventh-century Arabia, but that does not mean that either should still be permitted today. Similarly Taha, a Sudanese Sufi executed by Nimeiri, argued that the abiding message of the Quran is enshrined in the Meccan suras whereas the Medinan legislation was intended for a specific historical and geographical context. Such views are anathema to traditionalists and Islamists alike. Nevertheless, they often have considerable appeal to Muslims living in minority situations where the Quran's moral imperatives seem far more relevant than its legal injunctions.

13 Denominations and sects

Introduction

Some four fifths of the world's Muslims are Sunnis, and most of the remainder are Shiites. It is tempting, therefore, to think of Sunni Islam as the norm from which others have deviated. This would, however, be wrong on at least three counts. First, we should note that the situation has not always been as it is now. From about 950 to 1050, when the Buyid dynasty ruled most of Persia and Iraq, and the Fatimids held sway over North Africa, Cairo and Syria, it must have seemed to many that the whole of the Muslim world was on the verge of being won over to Shiism. Second, neither Sunni Islam nor Twelver Shiism existed in its full-blown form before the ninth century, for it was not until then that the principal Sunni Hadith collections were compiled and that the line of Shiite Imams came to an end. Third, the seeds from which Sunnism and Shiism grew were both present in the period of the rightly-guided Caliphs.

Sunnism and Shiism are essentially two different responses to the crisis caused when the Prophet Muhammad died without leaving clear instructions about who was to succeed him as leader of the community. In the face of this crisis, the majority, whom we may think of as proto-Sunnis, assumed that the era of the Prophet's charismatic authority was over and done with. They therefore sought a return to a routine stable life. In order to achieve this, they fell back on principles which had prevailed in pre-Islamic Arabia: respect for seniority, and the pre-eminence of the Quraish tribe. Thus the first four Caliphs were relatively aged long-standing Companions of the prophet, and they and all who succeeded them were drawn from the Quraish. Moreover, the proto-Sunnis viewed the Caliph in primarily political terms. With the passage of time the legal, religious and military leadership therefore devolved on other members of the community and were given carefully defined institutional forms. The response of the proto-Shiites to the Prophet's death was almost the exact opposite to this. They attempted to preserve his charismatic authority intact in a series of Imams who were his descendants. There was a third response, which proved less successful than either Sunnism or Shiism. This is the movement known as Kharijism. The Kharijites were fiercely egalitarian. They rejected both the return to pre-Islamic principles and the perpetuation of the Prophet's charismatic authority. In their view, the Caliph ought to be elected by the community as a whole and he could be any pious Muslim, Arab or non-Arab.

In the rest of this chapter, I propose to examine the three main branches of Shiism (Twelver, Ismaili and Zaydi) before looking briefly at Kharijism. I shall then give an account of the principal extant 'heresies'. Because Islam has neither church nor priesthood, deciding what is orthodox and what is heretical is not always easy. As a rule of thumb, I suggest that the criterion should be conformity to the *shahada*. Any movement which divinises a human being, or which alleges that God has sent another messenger after Muhammad, is heretical. On this definition, Kharijism is orthodox. so too are Twelver and Zaydi Shiism, despite their addition to the *shahada* of the words 'Ali is the Friend of God'. Ismaiili Shiism, which has taken on many different forms in the course of history, is however much more difficult to categorise, unlike the movements which will be discussed in the final section which are clearly beyond the pale of Islam.

Twelver Shiism

From the traditions preserved by the Sunnis and Shiites alike, it is evident that Ali, the first Shiite Imam, held a special place in the Prophet's affections. Ali was the Prophet's cousin and the wife of his daughter Fatima. Their sons Hasan and Hussein were his only grandchildren to reach adulthood. Consequently, on one occasion, he referred publicly to Ali, Fatima, Hasan and Hussein as his family. In addition to this, Ali acted as the Prophet's standard-bearer in a number of important campaigns, and when Ali expressed his disappointment at being left in charge in Medina during the expedition to Tabuk, he said to him

Are you not content to be in respect to me as Aaron was to Moses, except that after me there shall be no other prophet?

Finally, when the Prophet was returning to Medina after performing the pilgrimage for the last time, he stopped at Ghadir Khumm, took Ali's hand, and said that whoever looked on him, Muhammad, as his master, should view Ali in similar fashion. Shiites infer from these traditions, and others like them, that Ali, Fatima, Hasan and Hussein had a special status, and that the Prophet intended Ali to succeed him. The traditions are, however, tantalizingly ambiguous. All that we can say with confidence is that a few Muslims refused to swear allegiance to the first three Caliphs because of their belief that Ali was the Prophet's divinely-designated successor.

The Twelver Shiites regard Ali as the first of a series of twelve infallible Imams. The early history of Shiism is a highly controversial subject but there is no reliable evidence that the number of Imams was known in advance. On the contrary, when an Imam died there was a usually a dispute about whether or not the line had come to an end with him. The most serious crisis occurred when the eleventh Imam, Hasan al-Askari, died in 873, apparently without having a son to succeed him. His followers were split into at least fourteen groups. They disagreed about a variety of issues including whether or not he was really dead; whether or not he (or someone else) would return as the Mahdi; whether or not he had been succeeded by a twelfth Imam; and whether or not he had really died without issue. Within a hundred years or so, all these groups died out with the exception of the Twelver Shiites. They held that the twelfth Imam was Hasan al-Askari's son Muhammad, who was four years old when his father died. They alleged that for security reasons his birth had been kept secret; that he made a brief appearance to lead the funeral prayers for his father; and that he went into

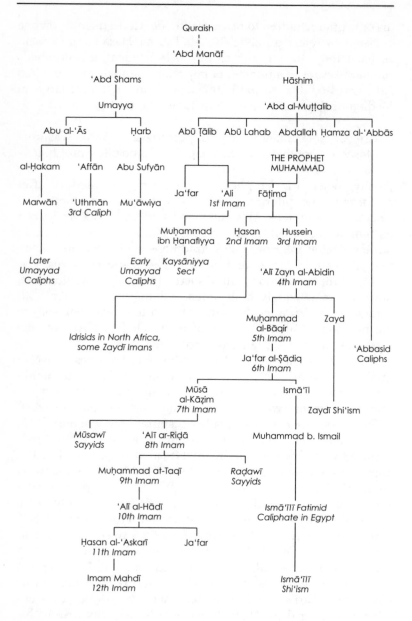

Figure 7 Genealogical Chart of the Shiite Imams

occultation or concealment. Between 874 and 941, the period of the Lesser Occultation, the twelfth Imam communicated with his followers through a series of four agents. In 941, with the onset of the Greater Occultation, all such communication ceased. Nevertheless, the Hidden Imam is still in control of human affairs and will reappear as the Mahdi shortly before the Day of Judgement.

Throughout history, the Shiite ulama have fluctuated between two opposing attitudes to politics. Sometimes they have appeared almost totally indifferent to temporal power and have been content merely to administer the religious law and to act as spiritual guides. At others, however, they have attempted to seize control politically in order to establish the rule of God. This tension was already present during the lives of the Imams. The second Imam, Hasan, relinquished his claim to political power, and most of his successors followed suit. However, his younger brother Hussein, the third Imam, died at Karbala in 680, resisting the tyranny of Yazid, the Umayyad Caliph. Shiites commemorate this event every year on the 10th of Muharram. On that day, they listen to recitals of Imam Hussein's suffering and participate in street processions in which they ritually re-enact his funeral. Ayatollah Khomeini used this powerful ritual to mobilize the Shiite masses during the Iranian revolution. He cast himself in the role of Imam Hussein, stigmatised the Shah as another Yazid, and equated those who were killed in the street demonstrations with the martyrs of Karbala.

Ismaili Shiism

According to Twelver Shiites, when the sixth Imam, Jafar as-Sadiq (d. 765), outlived his eldest son Ismail, whom he had designated to succeed him, he designated his second son, Musa al-Kazim, in his place. They therefore regard Musa as the seventh Imam and believe that the line continued through him. The early Ismailis, on the other hand, reserved a special role for Ali and held that the line of Imams began with his son Hasan. Thus, according to their reckoning, Jafar was the fifth Imam, not the sixth. They further maintained that Ismail did not die; that his father hid him out of fear for his safety; that he was the sixth Imam; and that his son Muhammad was the seventh. They had a cyclical view of history, dividing it into seven periods. Each period was inaugurated by a prophet who announced the external aspects of a revealed law. This enunciator (*natiq*) was succeeded by a legatee (*wasi*), who taught the inner meaning of the revelation to the spiritual elite. The legatee was in turn succeeded by seven Imams who guarded the true meaning of the revelations in both their external (*zahir*) and internal (*batin*) aspects. In each period, the seventh Imam rose to abrogate the previous *Sharia* and become the enuciator of the next. The enunciators of the first six periods were Adam, Noah, Abraham, Moses, Jesus and Muhammad. Their legatees were Seth, Shem, Ishmael, Aaron (or Joshua), Simon Peter, and Ali respectively. The seventh Imam of the sixth era was Muhammad b. Ismail. They held that he had gone into concealment, but that on his return he would be the Mahdi and would rule over the final era. He alone would unite the roles of enunciator and legatee; for instead of revealing a new *Sharia*, he would reveal the inner truths concealed behind all the previous messages – truths which had been grasped only partially by a spiritual elite.

Although relatively little is known about their early history, the Ismailis emerged from obscurity in the last quarter of the ninth century. In 873, Shiites were thrown into confusion when their eleventh Imam, Hasan al-Askari, died apparently without leaving an heir. Many of them were therefore receptive to the Ismaili claim that the line of Imams had in fact come to an end with Muhammad b. Ismail, and that he was about to return as the Mahdi. Thus, within twenty-five years, Ismaili propagandists succeeded in setting up cells throughout the Muslim world. One branch of the movement were known as the **Qarmathians**. In 894, they established a state in Bahrain. This continued to flourish until the end of the eleventh century. They pillaged Kufa and gained notoriety for attacking pilgrim caravans. In 929, they even sacked Mecca and carried off the black stone, reluctantly returning it twenty years later. Whereas the Qarmathians continued to await the return of seventh Imam, Muhammad b. Ismail, another branch, who subsequently adopted the name **Fatimids**, accepted the claim of their leader that he himself was the true Imam. In 909, he was declared Caliph in North Africa and took the throne-name al-Mahdi. The Fatimids modified the earlier teaching about the sixth era, the era of the Prophet

Muhammad. They argued that, unlike the previous eras, the sixth era had more than one series of seven Imams. Muhammad b. Ismail, the last of the first series, was succeeded by a second series, all of whom were hidden; these seven hidden Imams were succeeded in turn by the first seven Fatmid Caliphs, who were succeeded by a further seven. Moreover, the second heptad of Fatimid Caliphs were regarded as deputies of Muhammad b. Ismail and discharged some of his eschatological functions. Thus the onset of the final era of history receded further and further into the future.

When al-Mustansir, the eighth Fatimid Caliph, died in 1094, a dispute arose over which of his two sons should succeed him. The vizier installed al-Mustali, the younger of the two, and Nizar, his elder brother, had to flee for his life. Nizar and his son were subsequently murdered, but his infant grandson was allegedly smuggled to Persia. There thus arose a further schism: one group, known as the Mustalians, held that the imamate had passed to al-Mustali, while the other group, known as the Nizaris remained loyal to Nizar's descendants. The leadership of the **Nizaris** was assumed by Hasan-i Sabbah, a former Fatimid propagandist who had established a mountain stronghold at Alamut in Persia four years earlier. They also had a network of fortresses in Syria. Although there is no evidence that the Nizaris used narcotics, their Sunni opponents gave them the abusive nickname *Hashishiyyin* ('hashish users'), which passed into English as Assassins. At Hasan's instigation, they carried out some fifty or so political murders, hence the use of the word assassin to denote someone who deliberately kills a public figure. During Hasan's reign, and the reigns of his two successors, the identity of the Imams was not disclosed. However the fourth Lord of Alamut, Hasan II or Hasan ala dhikrihi s-salam ('Hasan on his mention be peace') claimed to be the Imam in person. Moreover, on Ramadan 17th 1164, he ordered his followers to stop fasting and he abolished the Sharia, publically declaring that the Day of Resurrection had arrived. Hasan II was succeeded in turn by his son and grandson, both of whom claimed the Imamate. However the grandson, Jalal ad-Din Hasan III, re-established the Sharia and attempted a rapprochement with the Sunnis. Alamut was sacked by the Mongols in 1256 and the Nizaris sank into relative obscurity until the nineteenth century, when the Shah of Persia gave the Nizari Imam the title Agha Khan ('Prince'). In 1852, after a subsequent rift with the Shah, the first Agha Khan took up residence in Bombay, where the Nizaris had been active for several centuries. The Nizaris of the Indian subcontinent sing hymns known as *ginans*. These hymns sometimes speak of the Imams in extravagant terms, deifying them and identifying them with Hindu avatars. The current leader of the Nizaris is Agha Khan IV, who is revered as the 49th Imam. Under his leadership, they have become much more orthodox.

The **Mustalians** recognised the Fatimid Caliph al-Mustali as Imam. After the murder of his successor in 1130, however, they split into two groups: the Hafizis and the Tayyibis. The former accepted the subsequent Fatimid Caliphs as Imams but died out soon after the dynasty came to an end. The latter believed in a series of hidden Imams. From 1130 to 1591 they established themselves in the Yemen. In 1591 they split into the Daudis and Sulaymanis. The Daudis are still thriving in parts of India, where they are commonly known as Bohoras.

Zaydism

The Zaydis trace their origin to Zayd, the son of the fourth Twelver Imam and half brother of the fifth. He held that it was not necessary for an Imam to be designated by his predecessor; the imamate could pass to any pious descendant of Hasan or Hussein who claimed it 'sword in hand'. He led a revolt against Caliph Hisham in 740 but was killed in battle. There were, however, several subsequent Zaydi uprisings: a Zaydi state was established in northern Iran from 913 to 1032, and another existed intermittently in the Yemen between 901 and 1962. Zaydis acknowledge the first four Twelver Imams but do not consider them infallible. They do not accept the existence of hidden Imams, and do not await a Mahdi. In theology they are Mutazilite but in other ways they are much closer to mainstream Sunnism: they recognise the caliphates of Abu Bakr and Umar and their legal system resembles the four Sunni law schools. There are some four million Zaydis in the Yemen.

Kharijism

The Kharijites first emerged at the battle of Siffin, when they objected to Ali's seeking arbitration on the grounds that judgement should be left to God alone. They then quit Ali's army, hence the name Kharijites (Arabic *khawarij*) which means those who secede. They were drawn from the poorest and most marginalised members of society and sought to establish a democratic system in which any Muslim, even an Abyssinian slave, could be elected Caliph. They put great stress on the moral purity of the Muslim community, whose members were the people of Paradise, and they therefore expelled sinners from their midst. Although they never succeeded in gaining control of any of the major cities, there were a number of Kharijite rebellions against oppression. In the eighth century, a moderate Kharijite group known as the Ibadis established a flourishing Berber state with its capital in Tahert in Western Algeria. Today, Ibadism is the official religion in Oman and there are small Ibadi communities in North Africa, notably in the Algerian oasis of Mzab and the Tunisian island of Jerba.

Beyond the Pale of Islam

The **Nusayris** probably originated among the Twelver Shiites in the suburbs of tenth-century Baghdad. They are named after Muhammad b. Nusayr an-Namiri, who was a pupil of the eleventh Imam, but their actual founder is now thought to have been al-Khasibi. They deify Ali and believe in the transmigration of souls although they try to pass themselves off as Shiites by adopting the name Alawis, 'followers of Ali'. President Asad of Syria is a Nusayri and they are politically dominant in his country, where they are mostly settled around Latakia.

The **Druze** religion is an offshoot of Ismailism, which originated in eleventh-century Egypt, during the reign of the sixth Fatimid Caliph, al-Hakim bi-Amr Allah. It is named after Muhammad b. Ismail al-Darazi, who preached that al-Hakim was divine. According to Druze doctrine, the Creator withdrew from mankind after Adam's fall but reincarnated himself in the Fatimid Caliphs. Al-Hakim's mysterious disappearance, while out riding one night in 1021, signified that the Creator had again withdrawn. The Druze were persecuted by the Fatimids but have survived to this day in central Lebanon and southern Syria. The majority do not know their scripture or the secrets of their own religion, which are only divulged to a select group of initiates.

The **Bahai** religion originated in nineteenth-century Iran and is an offshoot of Babism, which was itself an offshoot of Twelver Shiism. In 1844, the year 1260 of the Islamic era, that is to say by Muslim reckoning a thousand years after the onset of the Lesser Occultation, Sayyid Ali Muhammad Shirazi claimed to be the *Bab* or Gate of the Hidden Imam. Then, in 1848, he went much further and claimed that he was the returned twelfth Imam in person, and that he had come to abrogate the *Sharia*. He was executed in 1850, but not before he had appointed a successor to lead his followers, who were known as Babis, and had prophesied the advent of a person whom he referred to as 'Him whom Allah shall make manifest'. In 1866, Mirza Husayn Ali (1817–1892) publically claimed to be this messianic figure, and took the title Bahaullah ('Glory of Allah'). Most of the Babis accepted his claim and became Bahais. The Bahai religion subsequently spread to India, Europe and the Americas. The Bahais have their own scriptures and regard the Bab and Bahaullah as prophets of equal status with Muhammad.

The **Ahmadiyya** movement originated in late nineteenth-century India and is named after its founder, Mirza Ghulam Ahmad al-Qadiani (1839–1908), who came from Qadian in the Punjab. Their opponents refer to them as Qadianis or Mirzais. The movement is best understood as a syncretistic counterthrust to Hindu and Christian missionary activity, and an attempt to reach a compromise between traditionalist and modernist Islam. In response to the Arya Samaj Hindu revivalist movement, Ghulam Ahmad claimed that he was an incarnation of the Hindu god Krishna. His response to Christian missionary activity was more elaborate. The Christians poured scorn on the Muslim belief that a look-alike substitute was crucified in Jesus' place, after Jesus had ascended alive into heaven, and they proclaimed instead their faith in Jesus' death on the cross and his subsequent resurrection. Mirza Ghulam Ahmad admitted that Jesus had indeed been crucified, but alleged that he had been taken down from the cross while still alive and had found his way to

Kashmir, where he died and was buried. What is more, he alleged that he himself fulfilled the role of the risen Jesus. The Ahmadis are traditionalists in their attitude to polygamy and the seclusion of women, but they have embraced elements of Sayyid Ahmad Khan's modernism, including his denial that the Quran refers to miracles. They support obedience to the established political authorities holding that now, in the era of peace inaugurated by the advent of Ghulam Ahmad as the Messiah, *jihad* must take the form of missionary activity. They have met with considerable success in Africa, Asia and Europe, where they encourage people to read the Quran in their own highly tendencious translations. In Pakistan, they are not allowed to call themselves Muslims, because they revere their founder as a prophet. Nor are they permitted to perform the pilgrimage to Mecca.

The Lost-Found Nation of Islam is an American sect which originally had only tenuous links with Islam. It was founded in Detroit in 1930 by Wallace Fard, who claimed that he had come from Mecca to redeem the poor blacks and teach them that they were all of Muslim descent. After three years spent instructing his successor Elijah Poole, whose name he changed to Elijah Muhammad, Fard vanished, allegedly returning to Mecca. Members of the Nation of Islam are often referred to as Black Muslims. They hold extremely heterodox views. For them, Fard is God, and Elijah Muhammad is his prophet; blacks are all biological descendants of God, whereas whites are the creation of an evil scientist; and the hereafter will take place on earth after all the whites have been exterminated. When Elijah Muhammad died in 1975, leadership of the sect passed to his son Wallace. Wallace changed his name to Warith, not wishing to be associated with Wallace Fard. He repudiated the sect's racist doctrines, renamed it the World Community of al-Islam in the West, and attempted to turn its members into good Muslims. In 1979 a breakaway group led by Louis Farrakhan revived the original name and doctrines. The following year Warith renamed the parent body the American Muslim Mission.

The Arabic Language and Islamic Names

Arabic in Transliteration

When I have needed to mention Arabic words or expressions, I have usually transliterated them in the simplest possible way without using letters which are not found in the Roman alphabet or placing dots beneath consonants or macrons above vowels. For example, I have given the fourth Caliph's name as Ali rather than ʿAlī, and I have called the month of fasting Ramadan rather than Ramaḍān. If you read more advanced books, however, you will encounter several different systems of transliteration which correspond more accurately to the Arabic sounds. This can be rather bewildering for the non-Arabist but it is not as complicated as you might imagine. The following notes should help you. I shall begin by describing the most common system before going on to mention some important variations.

The Arabic alphabet comprises twenty-eight consonants which are usually transliterated as follows:

ʾ b t th j ḥ kh d dh r z s sh ṣ ḍ ṭ ẓ ʿ gh f q k l m n h w y.

In addition, Arabic has six vowels which are printed in religious texts and school books but which are otherwise omitted because the readers are expected to supply them from their knowledge of how the language works. Ths my sm dd t y (This may seem odd to you) but Arabs are used to it. In transliteration, however, the vowels are usually supplied. They are:

a i u ā ī ū.

For convenience we may divide these thirty-four sounds into eight groups:

1 Fifteen consonants which are pronounced almost exactly as in English. They are:

b t d r z s sh f k l m n h w y.

2 Three others which correspond closely to sounds that are common in English:

th is pronounced like the th in thank and think.
j is pronounced like the g in gem and gelatine.
dh is pronounced like the th in this, these and those.

3 Four emphatic consonants – *ṣ ṭ ḍ ẓ* – that do not occur in English. They are similar to *s t d z* but are pronounced with the tongue pressed against the edge of the upper teeth and then withdrawn forcefully.

4 Five guttural sounds - *ḥ kh ᶜ gh q* - that do not occur in standard English:

ḥ is more strongly aspirated and rasping than *h*.
kh is pronounced like ch in loch.
ᶜ is produced by compressing the throat and forcing up the larynx. If this makes you feel like retching you are probably making the right noise!
gh is the sound you make when gargling, like a French r but more throaty.
q is like *k* but pronounced further back in the throat.

6 The sign ᵓ which represents the light breathing that occurs in southern English at the beginning of words such as *a*wful and *a*bsolutely when they are given special emphasis.

7 The three short vowels:

a which is pronounced like the a in Englishman
i which is pronounced like the i in did.
u which is pronounced like the u in bull.

8 The three long vowels:

ā which is pronounced like the a in father.
ī which is pronounced like the ee in feet.
ū which is pronounced like the oo in room.

In the remaining sections of this appendix, I shall use this system to help familiarise you with it, but first we must look briefly at some other systems that you are likely to encounter.

The system of transliteration used in *The Encyclopaedia of Islam* differs from the above in three respects: *th, kh, dh, sh* and *gh* are printed as *th̲, kh̲, dh̲, sh̲* and *gh̲* to indicate that each pair represents a single Arabic consonant; *j* is shown as *dj̲*; and *q* is shown as *ḳ*. So if you want to know about the jinn, you will need to search the entries beginning with d, because the word is transliterated as *dj̲inn*. Similarly, if you wish to learn more about the Quran you must look under k because it is transliterated as *Ḳurʾān*.

Transliteration in **books published in India and Pakistan** is often influenced by Urdu pronounciation. Thus the letters ʿ and ʾ, and the dots beneath consonants are omitted; the long vowels are shown as *aa, ee* and *oo*; *u* sometimes becomes *o*; the letters *z, ẓ, dh* and *ḍ* all become *z*; *w* sometimes becomes *v*; and *th* becomes *s*. For example, you are likely to encounter *zikr* for *dhikr*; *hadees* for *ḥadīth*; and Omar for ʿUmar;.

In books written in or translated from **French** *j* is often transliterated *dj*; the long vowels may appear as *â, î, û*; and *sh* as *š* or *ch*. (Remember that in French words, *ch* is always pronounced *sh*. Quelle vie de chien! What a dog's life!).

In books written in or translated from **German**, *j* may be transliterated *dj* or *g*; *kh* as *ch*; and *y* as *j*. (Remember that, in written German, *j* represents the same sound as the English *y*. Ja naturlich! Yes of course!)

Some Hints about the Arabic Language

The definite article (English 'the') is represented by the prefix *al-*. There are two things you need to know about it. The first is that if the word to which it is prefixed begins with *t, th, d, dh, r, z, s, sh, ṣ, ḍ, ṭ, ẓ*, or *n*, the *l* of the article is pronounced the same as the letter in question. For example, the Arabic word for 'the sun' is pronounced *ash-shams* despite the fact that it is spelled *al-shams*. In the body of the book, my transliteration usually indicates the correct pronunciation, but you will find that many other authors invariably transliterate the article as *al-*, regardless of whether or not that is how it is pronounced. The second thing you need to know is that if a noun is followed by a genitive it does not have the article. Thus 'the Sun of the Religion' (a fairly common Arab name) is *Shams ad-Dīn*, not *ash-Shams ad-Dīn*.

In Arabic, some nouns are masculine and others are feminine. Most **feminine singular nouns** end in *-ah*. As the *h* is not actually pronounced, however, it is not always written in transliteration. For instance, you will encounter both *sunnah* and *sunna*, and both *surah* and *sura*. There is an additional peculiarity: when the feminine noun is followed by a word beginning with a vowel, the *h* is pronounced as a *t*. For example the second sura is called *surat al-baqara*, 'the Sura of the Cow'.

In English, most nouns may be put into the plural by simply adding an s – tradition, traditions; scholar, scholars and so forth. Some Arabic nouns behave in a similar way: if they are masculine they have a plural in *-ūm*, and if they are feminine they have a plural in *-āt*. However, many Arabic nouns have what are known as **broken plurals**. That is to say they undergo internal changes. For example, the plural of *'ālim* (religious scholar) is *'ulamā'*, and the plural of *ḥadīth* (tradition) is *aḥādīth*. When writing about Islam, some authors give the broken plural in transliteration but others simply add s or -s to the singular. So you will encounter *aḥādīth*, *ḥadīth*s and *ḥadīth*-s all meaning the same thing.

Most Arabic words are derived from **triliteral roots**. For example, *jihād* (struggle against unbelief), *mujāhid* (a person who engages in *jihād*), *ijtihād* (the exercise of independent judgement in questions of law); and *mujtāhid* (a person qualified to practise *ijtihād*), are all derived from the root *jhd*, which expresses the idea of self-exertion. When you come across long words which you are unfamiliar with, try to spot their root. This will help you both to understand them and to remember them.

Islamic Names

Muslim names can be quite bewildering. Before we examine their structure let me give you **an important tip**. Many names include the words Abu, Ibn or ʿAbd. These words mean Father, Son and Slave respectively. So never call anyone simply by one of them as if it were his first name! Likewise, never call him by the word which occurs immediately after Abū, Ibn or ʿAbd, for in the first case it is likely to be the name of his elder son; in the second, the name of his father; and in the third, one of the names of God! Classical Islamic names may have as many as **five or six components**. They are usually, but not invariably, given in the following order. First, there is the *kunya* or agnomen which designates the person as the father or mother of his or her eldest son. For example Abu Mūsa (Father of Mūsa), Umm Salama (Mother of Salama). Second, there is the *ism* or personal name. This is often the name of someone mentioned in the Qur'ān such as Mūsa, Yūsuf or Yūnus; or the name of the Prophet or one of his Companions: Muḥammad, ʿUmar, Ḥasan and so on. Quite frequently, however, it is a compound of ʿAbd and one of the names of God: ʿAbd Allāh (also written Abdullāh), ʿAbd al-Raḥmān (also written Abdurrahman) and so on. Third, the *ism* may be enlarged by a *laqab* with *ad-dīn*. For example Nūr ad-dīn, Shams ad-Dīn, or Fakhr ad-dīn (literally the Light of the Religion, the Sun of the Religion, and the Boast of the Religion). Fourth, there is the *nasab* or lineage. This indicates the person's relations with his forefathers over the past one, two or three generations: Ibn Aḥmad (Son of Aḥmad), Ibn Aḥmad ibn ʿAbd Allāh (Son of Aḥmad Son of ʿAbd Allāh), Ibn Aḥmad ibn ʿAbd Allāh ibn Yūsuf (Son of Aḥmad Son of ʿAbd Allāh Son of Yūsuf). Note that, when not the forst word, ibn is often abbreviated to b., for example Ibn Aḥmad b. ʿAbd Allāh. Fifth, there is the *nisba* or relation. This refers to the place of birth, residence or origin. It usually has the form al- + the name of the city + -i. For example, al-Bagdhādī. Last of all comes the *laqab* or nickname. This may be bestowed posthumously or during the person's lifetime; it may be honorific, or an insult; or it may simply indicate his trade, or one of his physical characteristics which helps distinguish him from other people with the same name.

Now let us look at **some examples**. Abū Jaʿfar Muḥammad ibn Jarīr al-Ṭabarī, was a famous historian and quranic commentator. His name consists of *kunya* + *ism* + *nasab* + *nisba*. Abu ʿAbd Allāh Muḥammad ibn Ismāʿīl al-Bukhārī, compiled the most important collection of ḥadīths. His name consists of the same four elements. However, Abu al-Ḥusayn ʿAsākir ad-dīn Muslim ibn al-Hajjāj ibn Muslim al-Qushayrī al-Nisabūrī, the name of the scholar who compiled the second most important collection, is more complex. It consists of *kunya* + *laqab* + *ism* + 2-generation *nasab* + 2 *nisbas*. The first *nisba* indicates that he belonged to the Qushayr tribe of the Arabs, whereas the second indicates that he was a native of Nisapur. The name of the famous Basran polymath ʿAmr ibn Baḥr al-Baṣrī al-Jāḥiẓ has four components: *ism* + *nasab* + *nisba* + *laqab*.

You may be wondering **how names are indexed**. There is no hard and fast rule but it is customary to list a person by the most well-known element of his name. This, of course, varies. Of the four persons whom I have just mentioned, the first two are known by their *nisbas*: al-Ṭabarī and al-Bukhārī. As the definite article is ignored for the purpose of indexing, you will find them listed under T and B respectively. However, the third person is known by his *ism*: Muslim, and the fourth by his *laqab*: al-Jāḥiẓ (literally, 'the boggle-eyed'). All this is not as mind-boggling as it may seem, for the simple reason that names are rarely given in full. Therefore you should not encounter too many difficulties.

The Islamic Calendar and Festivals

The Principle of the Lunar Calendar

There are three natural units which one may take into account when drawing up a calendar:

1 The terrestial day, the period of twenty-four hours that it takes the earth to complete a single revolution on its own axis.
2 The lunar month, the period of just over twenty-nine and a half days that it takes the moon to complete a single revolution round the earth.
3 The solar year, the period of slightly less than three hundred and sixty-five and a quarter days that it takes the earth to revolve round the sun.

Unfortunately, if you try to divide three hundred and sixty-five and a quarter by twenty-nine and a half, you are left with a remainder. Hence the calendarist is faced with an awkward choice: he can reckon in lunar months or solar years but he cannot easily reckon in both.

The pre-Islamic Arabs operated with a calendar of twelve lunar months, and refrained from shedding one another's blood during four of them which they regarded as especially sacred. The sacred months were: Rajab, during which they performed *umra*; Dhu 'l-Hijja, during which they performed *hajj*; and the months either side of Dhu 'l-Hijja, during which pilgrims from far afield would travel to and from the sacred sites around

Mecca. Every two or three years, they inserted a thirteenth month in order to keep the lunar year in relation to the solar year and the agricultural seasons. However, because they did not have a fixed system of intercalation but simply inserted a thirteenth month when they deemed it necessary, intercalation could be used to one group's advantage because it effectively postponed the arrival of the next sacred month. The Quran resolves the issue by prohibiting intercalation

> Surely the reckoning of months in the sight of Allah is twelve months, in accordance with His decree when He created the heavens and the earth, and of them four are sacred. That is the eternal religion so do not wrong each other in them. . ..Postponement of the sacred months by intercalation is an addition to unbelief. The unbelievers are led to wrong thereby, for they make it lawful one year and forbidden another year. . .
>
> (9.36f)

The obvious disadvantage of the lunar calendar is that it does not correspond to the agricultural seasons. Nevertheless, this is outweighed by three important considerations. First, in breaking with the solar year, the lunar calendar serves to counteract the human temptation to worship the sun and regard it as all-important. Second, annual fixtures, such as the month of fasting and the thirteen days of pilgrimage, migrate through the seasons, with the result that in the course of a lfetime the believer experiences them under a wide range of climatic conditions, learning to serve God faithfully in all of them. Third, the lunar calendar does not require complex calculations; 30-day months alternate with 29-day months and the beginning of each month is marked by the appearance of the slender crescent of the new moon.

The Muslim Year and Festivals

The Muslim year consists of twelve lunar months. Strictly speaking, there are only two Islamic festivals: *id al-adha*, 'the sacrificial festival', and *id al-fitr*, 'the festival of breaking fast'. The former, which is also known as *al-id al-kabir*, 'the great festival', occurs at end of the *hajj*. While the pilgrims are offering their sacrifices at Mina to commemorate the supreme sacrifice offered by Abraham and his son, every Muslim household throughout the world sacrifices a lamb or a sheep, distributing two-thirds of it as alms and eating the rest. The latter, which is also known as *al-id al-saghir*, 'the little festival', celebrates the end of the fast of *Ramadan*. Both festivals usually last for three or four days. They are marked by general feasting and rejoicing, the exchanging of gifts, and the wearing of new clothes. Instead of the normal dawn prayers, the believers perform two *rakas* in congregation, preferably out of doors, and listen to a sermon.

In addition to the two official festivals, many Muslims celebrate the Prophet's birthday (*mawlid an-nabi*) although Sunnis and Shiites disagree over the date on which it occurred. The most important specifically Shiite fixture is the commemoration of the death of Imam Hussein at Karbala. Shiites also commemorate the deaths of the other Imams, and the Prophet's designation of Ali as his successor at Ghadir Khumm. In many Muslim countries there are popular local festivals in honour of saints. A saint's festival is held on the anniversary of his death, the day when his soul was finally united with God. It is referred to as his *urs*, literally his 'wedding'.

The following table lists the twelve lunar months and indicates the dates of the two festivals together with other highlights of the Muslim year. Specifically Shiite commemorations are marked with an asterisk.

1 Muharram
      1–10, Martyrdom of third Imam, Hussein, at Karbala*
      9–10, Tasua & Ashura (culmination of Karbala commemorations)*
2 Safar
3 Rabia al-Awwal
      12, Birthday of Prophet
      17, Birthday of Prophet and of the sixth Imam, Jafar as-Sadiq*
4 Rabia al-Thani
5 Jumada al-Ula
6 Jumada al-Akhira

 7 Rajab
 8 Shaban
      15, Middle of Shaban
 9 Ramadan (*obligatory month-long fast*)
      21, Death of first Imam, Ali*
      27, Night of Power
10 Shawwal
      1–3, *id al-fitr*
11 Dhu l-Qada
12 Dhu l-Hijja
      8–10, *hajj*
      10–13, *id al-adha*
      18, Ghadir Khumm*

The Era of the Hijra: How to Convert Dates

In 622 AD, on September 10 or thereabouts, the Prophet left
Mecca and went to Medina. His departure from Mecca is known
as the *Hijra*, the Arabic word for Migration. The Era of the *Hijra*
is deemed, however, to have begun not on the precise day when
he left Mecca but on the first day of the Islamic year in which he
migrated. This occurred almost two months earlier, on July 16th.
Thus, 16 July 622 AD (AD = Anno Domini, the year of the Lord)
coincides with 1 Muharram 1 AH (AH = Anno Hijrae, the year of
the Hijra). If you have a date in the Christian or Common Era
calendar and wish to know the rough equivalent in the Islamic or
Hijri calendar, simply subtract 622. Note, however, that your
answer will be only a rough approximation because the Muslim
year is eleven days shorter than a solar year and there are
consequently 33 Muslim years to every 32 years in the Christian
calendar. To convert dates more accurately, it is therefore
necessary to use the following formulae:

$$AH = AD - 622 + \frac{AD - 622}{32} \qquad\qquad AD = AH + 622 - \frac{H}{33}$$

If for a specific date in one calendar you wish to know not only
the equivalent year but also the equivalent day and month in the

other calendar, the task of conversion will be much more difficult. There are three reasons for this. First, because a natural lunar month lasts just over twenty-nine and a half days, the Muslims found it necessary to have *kabisa* years in which they added an extra day. The system they opted for was to add a thirtieth day to the twelfth month of the 2nd, 5th, 7th, 10th, 13th, 14th, 16th, 19th, 22nd, 24th and 27th years of every 32-year cycle. Second, because a natural solar year lasts approximately three hundred and sixty-five and a quarter days, the Christians found it necessary to have leap years in which they added an extra day. The system they opted for was to add a twenty-ninth day to the second month at the turn of every century and every fourth year thereafter (1400, 1404, 1408, 1412, 1416 etc.). Third, because a natural solar year is in fact slightly less than three hundred and sixty-five and a quarter days, the Christian calendar gradually became out of step with the solar calendar and by 1582 it was ten days in advance. Pope Gregory XIII therefore ordered that ten days should be omitted from October of that year so that 4.10.1582 was followed immediately by 15.10.1582. Moreover, to prevent future errors from accumulating, Gregory decreed that centenary years whose first two figures were not divisble by four should not be leap years. Thus 1600 and 2000 were to be leap years but not 1700, 1800 and 1900. Most of Europe immediately adopted the Gregorian calendar but England retained the older Julian calendar until 1752 and it is still used for religious purposes in Russia. Fortunately, it is not necessary to engage in complex arithmetic every time you wish to convert a date. The answer can be found relatively quickly by consulting the tables in the book by G. S. P. Freeman-Grenville which is listed in the bibliography.

Select Bibliography

If you have access to a good reference library, you will be able to gain much valuable information from encyclopaedias. M. Eliade (ed.), *The Encyclopedia of Religion* (New York: Macmillan, 1987) contains a number of excellent articles on Islam and is often the best starting point. John L. Esposito (ed.), *The Oxford Encyclopedia of Islam in the Modern World* (New York: OUP, 1995) is also aimed at the general reader. For more advanced study, H. A. R. Gibb et al. (eds.), *The Encyclopaedia of Islam* (Leiden Brill, 1970-) is indispensable. To consult it, you will need to know the Arabic term for the subject which interests you and to understand the somewhat idiosyncratic system of transliteration which is employed (see Appendix 1). For rapid reference, Ian Richard Netton, *A Popular Dictionary of Islam* (London: Curzon, 1992) is invaluable.

Chapters 1 & 2. There is an extensive literature on European perceptions of Islam. The most accessible account of the early period is R. W. Southern, *Western Views of Islam in the Middle Ages* (Cambridge, Massachusetts: Harvard University Press, 1962); for a balanced survey which continues the story down to the twentieth century, Maxime Rodinson, *Europe and the Mystique of Islam* (London: I. B. Tauris, 1988) is thoroughly recommended.

Chapters 3 & 4. For annotated lists of the principal dynasties, consult C. E. Bosworth, *The Islamic Dynasties* (Edinburgh: EUP, 1967). The most satisfactory one-volume history of Islam is Ira M. Lapidus, *A History of Islamic Societies* (Cambridge: CUP, 1988). Ideally, it should be read in conjunction with William C. Brice (ed.), *An Historical Atlas of Islam* (Leiden: E. J. Brill, 1981) and

Francis Robinson, *Atlas of the Islamic World since 1500* (Oxford & New York: Facts on File, 1982). On the principal Islamist movements the following three books are recommended: G. Kepel, *The Prophet and Pharaoh: Muslim Extremism in Egypt* (London: Al-Saqi, 1985); S. V. R. Nasr, *The Vanguard of Islamic Revolution: The Jama'at-i Islami of Pakistan* (Berkley: University of California Press, 1994); and Suha Taji-Farouki, *A Fundamental Quest: Hizb al-Tahrir and the Search for Islamic Caliphate* (London: Grey Seal, 1996).

Chapter 5. The most useful general introduction to quranic studies is still W. Montgomery Watt, *Bell's Introduction to the Qur'an* (Edinburgh: EUP, 1970) although there have been a number of important developments since it was written. On the chronology of the revelations and the literary structure of the Quran see Neal Robinson, *Discovering the Qur'an: A Contemporary Approach to a Veiled Text* (London: SCM, 1996). For an introduction to classical exegesis which focuses on the quranic teaching about Jesus see Neal Robinson, *Christ in Islam and Christianity* (London: Macmillan, 1991). There is no detailed study of Quran translations but see Neal Robinson, 'Sectarian and Ideological Bias in English Translations of the Qur'an', *Islam and Christian-Muslim Relations* 8 (1997) 261–78.

Chapter 6. Ian Richard Netton, *Allah Transcendant: Studies in the Structure and Semiotics of Islamic Philosophy, Theology and Cosmology* (London: Routledge, 1989) is an excellent study of the various ways in which Muslims have thought of God, but it will be more readily appreciated by advanced students. The most accessible introduction to Islamic philosophy is M. Fakhry, *A History of Islamic Philosophy* (New York, 1983). There are many good books on Sufism but Annemarie Schimmel, *Mystical Dimensions of Islam* (Chapel Hill: University of North Carolina Press, 1975) is the best and most comprehensive.

Chapter 7. There is a need for a new critical biography of the Prophet but W. Montgomery Watt, *Muhammad: Prophet and Statesman* (Oxford OUP, 1961) is still serviceable. For those who wish to understand the place of Muhammad in Islamic piety, Annemarie Schimmel, *And Muhammad is His Messenger* (Lahore: Vanguard, 1987), is essential reading. Neal Robinson *The Sayings of Muhammad* (London: Duckworth, 1991) contains a selection of hadiths translated into good idiomatic English. The best introduction to hadith literature is M. Z. Siddiqi *Hadith Literature: Its Origin, Development & Special Features* (Cambridge: Islamic Texts Society, 1993). On non-Muslim hadith criticism see especially G. H. A. Juynboll *Studies on the Origins and Uses of Islamic Hadith* (London: Variorum, 1996).

Chapters 8–11. Al-Ghazali *Inner Dimensions of Islamic Worship* (Leicester: The Islamic Foundation, 1983) contains valuable insights into prayer, zakat, fasting and pilgrimage but the reader should bear in mind that the author died in 1111. On prayer, see the audiovisual tape and booklet: Neal Robinson, *Friday Prayers at the Mosque* (Leeds: Leeds University Television, 1993). There is much valuable information on the history of the pilgrimage in F. E. Peters, *The Hajj: The Muslim Pilgrimage to Mecca and the Holy Places* (Princeton: Princeton University Press, 1994).

Chapter 12. For a clear and detailed exposition of Islamic law written from a Sunni viewpoint see M. H. Kamali, *Principles of Islamic Jurisprudence*, revised edition (Cambridge: Islamic Texts Society, 1991). On the content of the Sharia, again from a Sunni viewpoint, see A. Rahman I. Doi, *Shar'iah: The Islamic Law*. For a brief history by a distinguished non-Muslim scholar see N. J. Coulson, *A History of Islamic Law* Edinburgh: EUP, 1989). There is as yet no good introduction to Shiite law in English. On the reform of law in the Muslim world, David Pearl, *A Textbook on Muslim Law* (London: Croom Helm, 1979) is excellent but rather dated.

Chapter 13. There are two excellent introductions to Shiism: Moojan Momen, *An Introduction to Shi'i Islam: the History and Doctrines of Twelver Shi'ism* (New Haven & London: Yale University Press, 1985) and Heinz Halm, *Shiism* (Edinburgh: EUP, 1991). The latter discusses both Twelvers and Ismailis. Farhad Daftery, *The Isma'ilis: Their history and doctrines* (Cambridge: CUP) is massive but very readable.

Appendix 1. See further Annemarie Schimmel, *Islamic Names* (Edinburgh: EUP, 1989).

Appendix 2. Conversion tables are furnished by G. S. P. Freeman-Grenville, *The Islamic amd Christian Calendars AD 622–2222 (AH 1–1650)*, 3rd edition (Reading: Garnet, 1995).

Index

Arabic names and technical terms are listed in alphabetical order in accordance with the simplified system of transliteration used in the body of the book. When appropriate, a more accurate transliteration is given in brackets. The Arabic definite article is ignored for indexing purposes. Thus, for example, al-Bistami will be found under B.

Subjects which are dealt with in a single discrete section of the book are not always listed. They may be located by reference to the subheadings in the Contents pages (pp. vii–x).